the happy time cocktail book

the happy time cocktail book

Illustrated by Tom Huffman

Gladstone Books
New York

Copyright © 1977 by Gladstone Books, Inc.
All rights reserved.
Printed in the United States of America.
Published by Gladstone Books, Inc., 218
Madison Avenue, New York, New York 10016.

Library of Congress Cataloging in Publication Data
Main entry under title:
The happy time cocktail book.
  Includes index.
  1. Cocktails. 2. Beverages.
TX951.H27   641.8'74   77-22326
ISBN 0-930150-01-5

CONTENTS

Introduction

The Happy Time Cocktail Book is a simple, straightforward guide to mixing beverages of all sorts at home. As you use this book, please remember that most recipes are merely guidelines—feel free to alter proportions, methods, garnishes, to suit your own personal tastes and style.

To make a drink from a particular kind of liquor, brandy, for instance, simply look in the table of contents, turn to the section containing brandy-based drinks, and leaf through till you find a recipe that strikes your fancy. If, on the other hand, you have a particular drink in mind, find the recipe you want by looking in the index.

Doodah, the blithe spirit who'll keep you company throughout this book, is the creation of well-known artist Tom Huffman. Doodah's humor is dry like a good martini, warm like a holiday toddy, and happy—like all your times should be.

Cheers.

Necessities

Although there are dozens of helpful and time-saving bar gadgets and appliances available, the following equipment will suffice to make the cocktails in this book.

- A *jigger measure* (1½ ounces) with accurate gradations for half ounces and quarter ounces.
- A combination *mixing glass and shaker*. Some recipes call for a blender; in virtually all cases, the drink can be made with a cocktail shaker and some energetic shaking.
- A *coil-rimmed strainer* for straining the ice out of a mixed cocktail as you pour it into a glass.
- A *set of measuring spoons*.
- A *long-handled mixing spoon*.
- A *measuring cup* is handy for making punches.

Measurements

Dash . . . . 1/6 teaspoon (1/32 ounce)
Teaspoon . . . . ⅛ ounce
Tablespoon . . . . 3 teaspoons; ½ ounce
Pony . . . . 1 ounce
Jigger . . . . 1½ ounces
Cup . . . . 8 ounces; ½ pint

Liquor Bottle Measurements

Miniature . . . . 1 ounce
Tenth . . . . 12.8 ounces (1/10 gallon)
Pint . . . . 16 ounces; ½ quart
Fifth . . . . 25.6 ounces; 4/5 quart; 1/5 gallon
Quart . . . . 32 ounces; ¼ gallon
Imperial quart . . . . 38.4 ounces

Wine Bottle Measurements (approximate)

Split . . . . 6 ounces; ¼ bottle
"Pint" . . . . 12 ounces; ½ bottle
"Quart" . . . . 24 to 26 ounces; 1 bottle
Magnum . . . . 52 ounces; 2 bottles
Jeroboam . . . . 104 ounces; 4 bottles

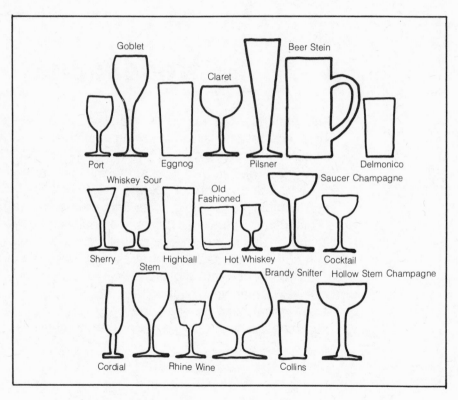

Aperitif, Beer, and Wine Cocktails

ABSINTHE

ABSINTHE SPECIAL

1½ OUNCES ABSINTHE
SUBSTITUTE
1 OUNCE WATER
½ TEASPOON SUGAR
2 DASHES ORANGE BITTERS

Shake all ingredients well with cracked ice and strain into a chilled cocktail glass.

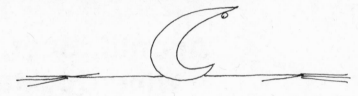

AMER PICON

AMER PICON COCKTAIL

1½ OUNCES AMER PICON
1 OUNCE LIME JUICE
1 TEASPOON GRENADINE

Shake all ingredients well with cracked ice and strain into a chilled cocktail glass.

BEER BUSTER

1½ OUNCES VODKA

LAGER *OR* ALE

1 OR 2 DASHES TABASCO SAUCE

Stir vodka with ice to chill and strain into a tall glass or stein. Add beer and Tabasco and stir gently.

BLOODY BEER

---

4 OUNCES TOMATO JUICE

DASH TABASCO SAUCE

SALT AND PEPPER

LAGER *OR* ALE

Place tomato juice, Tabasco, and salt and pepper in a chilled beer glass or stein; stir well. Fill glass with beer and stir gently.

HALF AND HALF (AMERICAN)

LAGER BEER
PORTER *OR* STOUT

Fill a chilled beer glass or stein halfway with lager. Fill the remainder of the glass with porter or stout; stir gently.

HALF AND HALF (ENGLISH)

LAGER BEER
ALE

Fill a chilled beer glass or stein halfway with lager. Fill the remainder of the glass with ale; stir gently.

LAGER AND LIME

LAGER BEER
ROSE'S LIME JUICE *OR*
FRESH LIME JUICE

Partially fill a chilled beer glass or stein with lager; add lime juice to taste and stir gently.

AMERICANO

1½ OUNCES CAMPARI
1½ OUNCES SWEET
VERMOUTH

Stir well with ice and strain into a chilled old-fashioned glass.
- **Serve with or without ice cubes.**
- **Garnish with a twist of lemon peel.**
- **In hot weather, pour over rocks in a tall glass and top off with club soda.**

NEGRONI

¾ OUNCE CAMPARI
¾ OUNCE GIN
¾ OUNCE SWEET VERMOUTH

Stir all ingredients well with cracked ice and strain into a chilled cocktail glass.
- **Garnish with a twist of lemon peel.**
- **In hot weather, pour drink over rocks in a tall glass and top off with club soda.**

13

ALFONSO

---

1 SMALL LUMP *OR*
½ TEASPOON SUGAR
DASH ORANGE BITTERS
1 OUNCE RED DUBONNET
CHILLED CHAMPAGNE

Put sugar in a large champagne glass and moisten with bitters. Add one or two cubes of ice, pour in the Dubonnet, and fill with champagne.
• Add a twist of lemon or orange peel.

BLACK VELVET (CHAMPAGNE VELVET)

---

5 OUNCES CHILLED STOUT
5 OUNCES CHILLED
CHAMPAGNE

Use a tall, 14-ounce glass. Slowly pour in stout, and then add champagne very carefully.

BUCKS FIZZ

---

3 OUNCES CHILLED
ORANGE JUICE
CHILLED CHAMPAGNE

Put orange juice in a tall glass and slowly add champagne; stir very carefully.

CHAMPAGNE COCKTAIL

1 SMALL LUMP *OR*
½ TEASPOON SUGAR
DASH ANGOSTURA BITTERS
CHILLED CHAMPAGNE
LEMON PEEL

Put sugar in a chilled champagne glass and moisten with dash of bitters. Add champagne; twist lemon peel over glass and drop in.

CHAMPAGNE COOLER

1 OUNCE BRANDY
1 OUNCE TRIPLE SEC *OR*
COINTREAU
¼ TEASPOON WHITE
CREME DE MENTHE
CHILLED CHAMPAGNE

Fill a tall glass halfway with crushed ice. Add all ingredients except champagne and stir. Fill with champagne.
● Decorate with a spiral of orange peel.

CHAMPAGNE PUNCH (FOR ONE)

1 OUNCE FRAMBOISE
1 TABLESPOON LEMON JUICE
CHILLED CHAMPAGNE

Fill a tumbler three-quarters full of cracked ice. Add framboise and lemon juice and fill with champagne; stir gently.

FRENCH 75

1½ OUNCES GIN
1 TABLESPOON LEMON JUICE
1 TEASPOON SUGAR
CHILLED CHAMPAGNE

Put gin, lemon juice, and sugar in a tall glass and stir until sugar is dissolved. Fill the glass halfway with cracked ice and slowly add champagne. Serve with straws, if you wish.
• Decorate with any of or all the following: lemon slice, orange slice, maraschino cherry.
• To make a French 95, substitute bourbon for the gin.
• To make a French 125, substitute brandy for the gin.

16

MONTE CARLO IMPERIAL

1½ OUNCES GIN
½ OUNCE WHITE CREME
DE MENTHE
1 TEASPOON LEMON JUICE
CHILLED CHAMPAGNE

Shake all ingredients except champagne well with cracked ice and strain into a highball glass or large wine glass. Fill with champagne and stir gently.

CREME DE CASSIS

BYRRH CASSIS

1½ OUNCES BYRRH
2 TEASPOONS
CREME DE CASSIS
1 TABLESPOON LEMON JUICE

Shake all ingredients well with cracked ice and strain over rocks in an old-fashioned glass.
● Garnish with a lemon slice or a twist of lemon peel.

17

GIN CASSIS

1½ OUNCES GIN
½ OUNCE CREME DE CASSIS
1 TABLESPOON LEMON JUICE

Shake well with cracked ice. Strain into chilled cocktail glass or over rocks in an old-fashioned glass.

KIR

3½ OUNCES DRY WHITE WINE
½ OUNCE CREME DE CASSIS

Stir well with ice and pour into a chilled wine glass or old-fashioned glass. Add ice, if you wish.

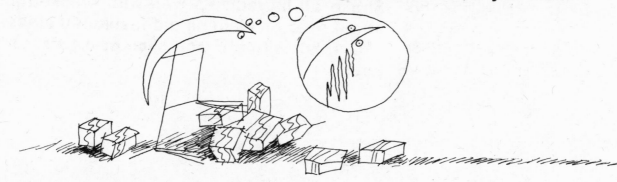

VERMOUTH CASSIS

2 OUNCES DRY VERMOUTH
½ OUNCE CREME DE CASSIS
CLUB SODA

Put two ice cubes in a highball glass, an old-fashioned glass, or a large wine glass. Pour in vermouth and crème de cassis. Add club soda and stir.
• Garnish with a lemon slice or a twist of lemon peel.
• To make a white-wine *(vin-blanc)* cassis, substitute dry white wine for the vermouth.

DUBONNET
DUBONNET COCKTAIL

1½ OUNCES RED DUBONNET
1 OUNCE GIN

Stir both ingredients well with cracked ice and strain into a chilled cocktail glass.
• Add a twist of lemon peel.

MERRY WIDOW

1¼ OUNCES RED DUBONNET
1¼ OUNCES DRY VERMOUTH
LEMON PEEL

Stir Dubonnet and vermouth with cracked ice and strain into a chilled cocktail glass. Twist lemon peel over glass and add.

SANCTUARY

1¼ OUNCES RED DUBONNET
½ OUNCE AMER PICON
½ OUNCE TRIPLE SEC
OR COINTREAU

Shake all ingredients well with cracked ice and strain into a chilled cocktail glass.

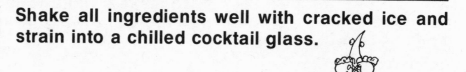

WEEP NO MORE

1 OUNCE RED DUBONNET
¾ OUNCE BRANDY
¾ OUNCE LEMON *OR*
LIME JUICE
DASH GRENADINE

Shake all ingredients well with cracked ice and strain into a chilled cocktail glass.

PORT WINE
BROKEN SPUR

1½ OUNCES WHITE PORT
¾ OUNCE SWEET VERMOUTH
2 DASHES CURACAO

Shake all ingredients well with cracked ice and strain into a chilled cocktail glass.

BROKEN SPUR II

1½ OUNCES WHITE PORT
2 TEASPOONS GIN
2 TEASPOONS SWEET
VERMOUTH
1 TEASPOON PERNOD
1 EGG YOLK

Shake all ingredients well with cracked ice and strain into a large goblet.

CHOCOLATE COCKTAIL

1½ OUNCES PORT
½ OUNCE YELLOW
CHARTREUSE
1 TEASPOON GRATED SWEET
COOKING CHOCOLATE

Shake all ingredients well with cracked ice and strain into a chilled cocktail glass.

DEVIL'S COCKTAIL

1¼ OUNCES PORT
1¼ OUNCES DRY VERMOUTH
2 DASHES LEMON JUICE

Shake all ingredients well with cracked ice and strain into a chilled cocktail glass.

PORT WINE COCKTAIL

2½ OUNCES PORT
½ TEASPOON BRANDY

Shake port and brandy well with cracked ice and strain into a chilled cocktail glass.

SHERRY
ADONIS

1½ OUNCES DRY SHERRY
¾ OUNCE SWEET VERMOUTH
DASH ORANGE BITTERS

Shake all ingredients well with cracked ice and strain into a chilled cocktail glass.
• Add a twist of lemon peel.

BAMBOO

1½ OUNCES DRY SHERRY
¾ OUNCE DRY VERMOUTH
DASH ORANGE BITTERS

Shake all ingredients well with cracked ice and strain into chilled cocktail glass.
- **Add a twist of lemon peel.**

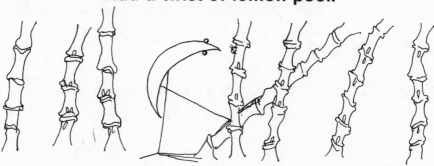

BRAZIL

1¼ OUNCES DRY SHERRY
1¼ OUNCES DRY VERMOUTH
DASH PERNOD
DASH ANGOSTURA BITTERS

Shake all ingredients well with cracked ice and strain into a chilled cocktail glass.
- **Add a twist of lemon peel.**

CUPID

3 OUNCES SHERRY
1 EGG
1 TEASPOON SUGAR
PINCH CAYENNE PEPPER

Shake all ingredients well with cracked ice and strain into a chilled highball or collins glass.

FINO

1½ OUNCES FINO SHERRY
1 OUNCE SWEET VERMOUTH

Stir well with ice. Serve over rocks in an old-fashioned glass.
● Garnish with a twist of lemon peel.

REFORM

1½ OUNCES SHERRY
¾ OUNCE DRY VERMOUTH
DASH ORANGE BITTERS

Shake all ingredients well with cracked ice and strain into a chilled cocktail glass.

25

SHERRIED ORANGE

1 OUNCE CREAM SHERRY
1 TABLESPOON BRANDY
1 OUNCE ORANGE JUICE
1 TABLESPOON CREAM

Shake all ingredients well with cracked ice and strain into a chilled cocktail glass.

SHERRY COCKTAIL

2½ OUNCES SHERRY
2 DASHES DRY VERMOUTH
DASH ORANGE BITTERS

Shake all ingredients well with cracked ice and strain into a chilled cocktail glass.
• Add a twist of orange peel or lemon peel.

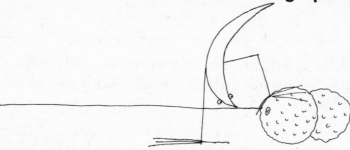

SHERRY TWIST

1 OUNCE SHERRY
2 TEASPOONS TRIPLE SEC OR
COINTREAU
2 TEASPOONS BRANDY
2 TEASPOONS DRY
VERMOUTH
GROUND CINNAMON

Shake all ingredients except cinnamon with cracked ice and strain into a chilled cocktail glass. Sprinkle with ground cinnamon.
● Add a twist of orange peel or lemon peel.

STONE

1½ OUNCES SHERRY
½ OUNCE LIGHT RUM
½ OUNCE SWEET VERMOUTH

Shake all ingredients well with cracked ice and strain into a chilled cocktail glass.

27

TUXEDO

2 OUNCES SHERRY
½ OUNCE ANISETTE
¼ TEASPOON MARASCHINO
LIQUEUR
DASH PEYCHAUD'S *OR*
ANGOSTURA BITTERS

Shake all ingredients well with cracked ice and strain into a chilled cocktail glass.

SWEDISH PUNCH
DOCTOR

1½ OUNCES SWEDISH PUNCH
¾ OUNCE LIME JUICE

Shake both ingredients well with ice and strain into a chilled cocktail glass.

GRAND SLAM

1½ OUNCES SWEDISH PUNCH
½ OUNCE DRY VERMOUTH
½ OUNCE SWEET VERMOUTH

Shake all ingredients well with cracked ice and strain into a chilled cocktail glass.

HESITATION

2¼ OUNCES SWEDISH PUNCH
½ OUNCE WHISKEY
LEMON PEEL

Stir Swedish punch and whiskey well with cracked ice. Strain into a chilled cocktail glass. Squeeze lemon peel over drink and add.

MAY BLOSSOM FIZZ

2 OUNCES SWEDISH PUNCH
1 TABLESPOON LEMON JUICE
1 TEASPOON GRENADINE
CLUB SODA

Shake all ingredients except club soda with cracked ice and strain into a highball glass that is half-filled with ice cubes. Top off with club soda.

WALDORF

1½ OUNCES SWEDISH PUNCH
¾ OUNCE GIN
¾ OUNCE LEMON *OR*
LIME JUICE

Shake all ingredients well with cracked ice and strain into a chilled cocktail glass.

BISHOP

1 TEASPOON LEMON JUICE
1 TEASPOON ORANGE JUICE
1 TEASPOON SUGAR
4 OUNCES DRY RED WINE

Put fruit juices and sugar into a highball glass and stir until sugar is dissolved. Fill glass halfway with cracked ice and pour in wine; stir.
• Decorate with a slice of lemon or orange.

HOT BUTTERED WINE

4 OUNCES WINE
2 OUNCES WATER
1 TEASPOON BUTTER
1 TABLESPOON MAPLE SYRUP
NUTMEG (OPTIONAL)

Heat wine and water just to boiling. Pour into heated mug or cup. Add butter and maple syrup; stir. Top with grated nutmeg, if desired.
● Add a cinnamon stick, if you wish.

HOT SPRINGS

1½ OUNCES DRY WHITE WINE
1 TABLESPOON
PINEAPPLE JUICE
½ TEASPOON
MARASCHINO LIQUEUR
DASH ORANGE BITTERS

Shake all ingredients well with cracked ice and strain into a chilled cocktail glass.

PINEAPPLE COOLER

2 OUNCES PINEAPPLE JUICE
½ TEASPOON SUGAR
2 OUNCES DRY WHITE WINE
CLUB SODA

In a collins or other tall glass, put pineapple juice and sugar and stir until sugar is dissolved. Fill glass with cracked or crushed ice, pour in wine, and stir; add ice to fill.

• Decorate with a slice of lemon or orange or a spiral of lemon or orange peel.

QUEEN CHARLOTTE

2 OUNCES DRY RED WINE
1 OUNCE RASPBERRY SYRUP
OR GRENADINE
1 TABLESPOON LEMON JUICE
1 TEASPOON SUGAR
CLUB SODA

Shake all ingredients except club soda well with cracked ice and strain into a collins glass that is half filled with cracked ice. Fill with club soda and stir.

• Garnish with a lemon slice and a cherry.

SPRITZER

3 OUNCES WHITE WINE
CLUB SODA

Fill a tall glass halfway with ice cubes or cracked ice. Pour in wine and add club soda to fill; stir.
- **Add a twist of lemon peel or a lemon slice.**
- **Although spritzers are traditionally made with white wines, red wines also work very well.**

WINE COBBLER

1 TEASPOON SUGAR
2 OUNCES CLUB SODA
4 OUNCES WINE

In a large goblet or a collins glass, dissolve the sugar in the club soda. Fill glass with crushed ice and pour in wine; stir. Add more crushed ice to fill, if necessary.
- **Decorate with lemon, lime, or orange slices, or with any fresh fruit.**

WINE EGGNOG

3 OUNCES WINE
4 OUNCES MILK
2 TEASPOONS SUGAR
1 EGG
NUTMEG (OPTIONAL)

Shake all ingredients except nutmeg well with cracked ice and strain into a chilled collins glass. Top with grated nutmeg, if desired.
● For an extra frothy eggnog, blend at high speed in a blender for 10 to 15 seconds.

WINE FLIP

1½ OUNCES WINE
1 TABLESPOON CREAM
1 EGG
1 TEASPOON SUGAR
NUTMEG (OPTIONAL)

Shake all ingredients except nutmeg well with cracked ice and strain into a chilled flip glass. Top with grated nutmeg, if desired.
● To make in a blender, blend 10 to 15 seconds at high speed.

34

WINE MILK PUNCH

3 OUNCES WINE
6 OUNCES MILK
1 TEASPOON SUGAR
NUTMEG (OPTIONAL)

Shake all ingredients except nutmeg with cracked ice and strain into a collins glass. Top with grated nutmeg, if desired.

WINE NEGUS

2 OUNCES WINE
½ TEASPOON SUGAR
BOILING WATER
NUTMEG (OPTIONAL)

Put wine and sugar in a hot whiskey glass, coffee cup, or mug and add boiling water to fill; stir. Top with grated nutmeg, if you wish.

35

WINE SANGAREE

1 TEASPOON WATER
½ TEASPOON SUGAR
2½ OUNCES WINE
CLUB SODA
1 TABLESPOON BRANDY
NUTMEG (OPTIONAL)

Put water and sugar in a highball glass and stir until sugar is dissolved. Add ice cubes or cracked ice to fill glass halfway. Pour in wine and fill with club soda, leaving just enough room to float brandy on top. Dust with grated nutmeg, if desired.

VERMOUTH
ADDINGTON

1½ OUNCES DRY VERMOUTH
1½ OUNCES SWEET
VERMOUTH
CLUB SODA

Pour dry and sweet vermouth into a highball glass half filled with ice. Top off with club soda and stir. ● Garnish with a slice of orange or lemon, or a twist of orange or lemon peel.

BONSONI

1½ OUNCES SWEET
VERMOUTH
¾ OUNCE FERNET BRANCA

Stir both ingredients well with cracked ice and strain into a chilled cocktail glass.

CRYSTAL BRONX

1 OUNCE DRY VERMOUTH
1 OUNCE SWEET VERMOUTH
¾ OUNCE ORANGE JUICE
CLUB SODA

Shake both vermouths and the orange juice well with cracked ice and strain into a highball or collins glass that is half filled with ice. Add club soda to fill; stir.
• Decorate with a spiral of orange or lemon peel.

DIPLOMAT

1½ OUNCES DRY VERMOUTH
¾ OUNCE SWEET VERMOUTH
¼ TEASPOON
MARASCHINO LIQUEUR

Shake all ingredients well with cracked ice and strain into a chilled cocktail glass.

FIG LEAF

1½ OUNCES SWEET
VERMOUTH
¾ OUNCE LIGHT RUM
1 TABLESPOON LIME JUICE
DASH ANGOSTURA BITTERS

Shake all ingredients well with cracked ice and strain into a chilled cocktail glass.

GREEN ROOM

1½ OUNCES DRY VERMOUTH
¾ OUNCE BRANDY
¼ TEASPOON CURACAO

Shake all ingredients well with cracked ice and strain into a chilled cocktail glass.

HARVARD WINE

1 OUNCE DRY VERMOUTH
½ OUNCE BRANDY
CLUB SODA

Shake vermouth and brandy well with cracked ice and strain into a chilled cocktail glass. Top off with club soda.
• Add a twist of lemon peel.

HUMPTY DUMPTY

1½ OUNCES DRY VERMOUTH
¾ OUNCE
MARASCHINO LIQUEUR

Shake both ingredients well with cracked ice and strain into a chilled cocktail glass.

PERPETUAL

1¼ OUNCES DRY VERMOUTH
1¼ OUNCES SWEET VERMOUTH
½ TEASPOON CREME DE VIOLETTE
¼ TEASPOON CREME DE CACAO

Shake all ingredients well with cracked ice and strain into a chilled cocktail glass.

VERMOUTH COCKTAIL

2½ OUNCES SWEET VERMOUTH
2 DASHES ANGOSTURA *OR* ORANGE BITTERS (OPTIONAL)
LEMON PEEL

Vermouth can be served as a cocktail or aperitif in several ways: 1) Stir vermouth and bitters well with ice and strain into a cocktail glass; 2) Fill a cocktail glass with crushed ice, add vermouth and bitters, and stir; 3) Fill an old-fashioned glass with ice cubes, add vermouth and bitters, and stir. In each of the three, squeeze the lemon peel over the drink and then drop it in.

Brandy Cocktails

APPLE BRANDY
APPLE BLOW FIZZ

---

2 OUNCES APPLE BRANDY
1 EGG WHITE
JUICE OF ½ LEMON
1 TEASPOON SUGAR
CLUB SODA

Shake all ingredients except club soda well with cracked ice and strain into chilled highball glass. Top off with club soda.
• Garnish with a lemon slice.

APPLEJACK COCKTAIL

1½ OUNCES APPLEJACK
½ OUNCE SWEET VERMOUTH
DASH ANGOSTURA BITTERS

Shake all ingredients well with cracked ice and strain into a chilled cocktail glass.
• Garnish with a marashino cherry, if desired.
• For a slightly different taste, substitute orange bitters for the Angostura bitters.

APPLEJACK RABBIT

1½ OUNCES APPLEJACK
1 TABLESPOON MAPLE SYRUP
1 TABLESPOON LEMON JUICE
1 TABLESPOON
ORANGE JUICE

Shake all ingredients well with cracked ice and strain into chilled cocktail glass.
● Frosting the glass with sugar makes this drink even tastier: Moisten the rim of the glass with lemon juice and dip in sugar.

APPLEJACK SOUR

2 OUNCES APPLEJACK
JUICE OF ½ LEMON
1 TEASPOON SUGAR

Shake all ingredients well with cracked ice and strain into a chilled sour glass.
● Garnish with a lemon slice and a maraschino cherry.

JACK ROSE

1½ OUNCES APPLEJACK
1 TABLESPOON LIME OR
LEMON JUICE
1 TEASPOON GRENADINE

Shake all ingredients well with cracked ice and strain into a chilled cocktail glass.

APRICOT BRANDY
AFTER-DINNER COCKTAIL

1½ OUNCES APRICOT BRANDY
1 OUNCE CURACAO
2 TABLESPOONS LIME JUICE

Shake all ingredients well with cracked ice and strain into a chilled cocktail glass.

APRICOT COOLER

2 OUNCES APRICOT BRANDY
1 TABLESPOON LEMON JUICE
1 TEASPOON SUGAR
CLUB SODA

Shake brandy, lemon juice, and sugar well with ice. Strain into a tall, ice-filled glass. Top off with club soda.

BREAKFAST EGGNOG

1½ OUNCES APRICOT BRANDY
½ OUNCE CURACAO
1 EGG
4 OUNCES MILK
NUTMEG (OPTIONAL)

Shake all ingredients except nutmeg well with cracked ice and strain into a chilled, tall glass. Top with grated nutmeg, if desired.

45

BLACKBERRY BRANDY

POOP DECK

1 OUNCE BLACKBERRY
BRANDY
½ OUNCE BRANDY
½ OUNCE PORT *OR* SHERRY

Shake all ingredients well with cracked ice and strain into a chilled cocktail glass.

CHERRY BRANDY

CHERRY BLOSSOM

1½ OUNCES CHERRY BRANDY
1 OUNCE BRANDY
DASH CURACAO
DASH GRENADINE
DASH LEMON JUICE

Shake all ingredients well with cracked ice and strain into a chilled cocktail glass.

46

CHERRY FIZZ

2 OUNCES CHERRY BRANDY
1 TABLESPOON LEMON JUICE
CLUB SODA

Shake well with cracked ice and strain into a chilled highball glass. Top off with club soda; stir.

BRANDY
ALABAMA

1½ OUNCES BRANDY
1 TEASPOON CURACAO
1 TABLESPOON LEMON JUICE
½ TEASPOON SUGAR

Shake all ingredients well with cracked ice. Strain into a chilled cocktail glass.
● Garnish with a twist of lemon or orange peel.

BOMBAY

1 OUNCE BRANDY
½ OUNCE SWEET VERMOUTH
½ OUNCE DRY VERMOUTH
½ TEASPOON CURACAO
¼ TEASPOON PERNOD

Shake all ingredients well with cracked ice and strain into chilled cocktail glass.

BRANDY ALEXANDER

1 OUNCE BRANDY
½ OUNCE CREME DE CACAO
1 OUNCE CREAM

Shake all ingredients well with cracked ice and strain into a chilled cocktail glass.

BRANDY GUMP

1½ OUNCES BRANDY
1 TABLESPOON LEMON JUICE
2 DASHES GRENADINE

Shake all ingredients well with cracked ice and strain into a chilled cocktail glass.

BRANDY SOUR

2 OUNCES BRANDY
1 TABLESPOON LEMON JUICE
1 TEASPOON SUGAR

Shake all ingredients well with cracked ice and strain into a chilled sour glass.
● Garnish with a cherry and a lemon and/or orange slice.

CHAMPS ELYSEES

1½ OUNCES COGNAC
½ OUNCE YELLOW
CHARTREUSE
1 TABLESPOON LEMON JUICE
½ TEASPOON SUGAR
DASH ANGOSTURA BITTERS

Shake all ingredients well with ice. Strain into a chilled cocktail glass or serve on the rocks in an old-fashioned glass.

CHICAGO

2 OUNCES BRANDY
2 DASHES CURACAO
DASH ANGOSTURA BITTERS

Shake all ingredients well with cracked ice and strain into a chilled cocktail glass.
● Before mixing the drink, rub the rim of the glass with lemon and dip into sugar.

CLASSIC

1½ OUNCES BRANDY
2 TEASPOONS CURACAO
2 TEASPOONS MARASCHINO
LIQUEUR
1 TABLESPOON LEMON JUICE

Shake all ingredients well with cracked ice and strain into a chilled cocktail glass.

COLD DECK

1½ OUNCES BRANDY
½ OUNCE WHITE CREME
DE MENTHE
½ OUNCE SWEET VERMOUTH

Shake all ingredients well with cracked ice and strain into a chilled cocktail glass.
• For a dry cold deck, substitute dry vermouth for the sweet.

DEAUVILLE

½ OUNCE BRANDY
½ OUNCE APPLE BRANDY
½ OUNCE TRIPLE SEC
1 TABLESPOON LEMON JUICE

Shake all ingredients well with cracked ice and strain into chilled cocktail glass.

FROUPE

1¼ OUNCES BRANDY
1¼ OUNCES SWEET
VERMOUTH
1 TEASPOON BENEDICTINE

Shake all ingredients well with cracked ice and strain into a chilled cocktail glass.

HARVARD

1½ OUNCES BRANDY
¾ OUNCE SWEET VERMOUTH
1 TABLESPOON LEMON JUICE
1 TEASPOON GRENADINE
DASH ANGOSTURA BITTERS

Shake all ingredients well with cracked ice. Strain into a chilled cocktail glass.

JAMAICA GRANITO

1½ OUNCES BRANDY
1 OUNCE CURACAO
SCOOP OF LEMON *OR*
ORANGE SHERBET
CLUB SODA
NUTMEG (OPTIONAL)

Place brandy, curaçao, and sherbet in a tall glass. Add club soda and stir. Dust with grated nutmeg.

PHOEBE SNOW

1¼ OUNCES BRANDY
1¼ OUNCES RED DUBONNET
2 DASHES PERNOD

Shake all ingredients well with cracked ice and strain into a chilled cocktail glass.

QUAKER

1 OUNCE BRANDY
1 OUNCE RUM
1 TABLESPOON LEMON JUICE
2 TEASPOONS
RASPBERRY SYRUP

Shake all ingredients well with cracked ice and strain into a chilled cocktail glass.
• Garnish with a lemon slice or a twist of lemon peel.

SARATOGA

2 OUNCES BRANDY
1 TEASPOON MARASCHINO
LIQUEUR
1 TABLESPOON PINEAPPLE
JUICE
1 TEASPOON LEMON JUICE
DASH ANGOSTURA BITTERS

Shake all ingredients well with cracked ice. Strain into chilled cocktail glass.

SIDECAR

1 OUNCE BRANDY
¾ OUNCE TRIPLE SEC
¾ OUNCE LEMON JUICE

Shake all ingredients well with cracked ice and strain into chilled cocktail glass.
● A sidecar can be made with almost any liquor: blended whiskey, Canadian whiskey, Irish whiskey, gin, tequila, rum, or Scotch in place of the brandy.

STINGER

1 OUNCE BRANDY
1 OUNCE WHITE CREME DE MENTHE

Shake brandy and crème de menthe well with cracked ice and strain into a chilled cocktail glass.
● Stingers are exceptionally versatile. They go well at brunch, before dinner, after dinner, or as a nightcap.
● You can substitute virtually any liquor for the brandy in this recipe.

WATERBURY

1½ OUNCES BRANDY
1 TABLESPOON LEMON JUICE
½ TEASPOON GRENADINE
1 EGG WHITE
½ TEASPOON SUGAR

Shake all ingredients well with cracked ice and strain into a chilled cocktail glass.
● Before mixing the drink, frost the rim of the glass by rubbing it with lemon and dipping it into sugar.

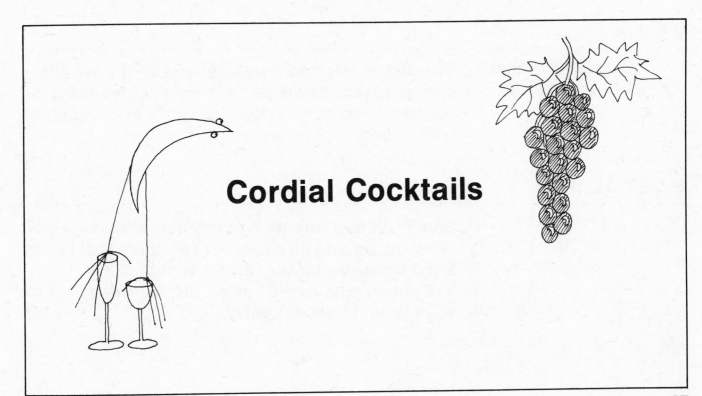

Cordial Cocktails

B & B

½ OUNCE BENEDICTINE
½ OUNCE COGNAC

The B & B is served several ways: 1) mixed in a cordial glass; 2) unmixed in a cordial glass with the cognac floated on top; 3) iced in a cocktail glass with a twist of lemon peel.

B & B COLLINS

1½ OUNCES COGNAC
½ OUNCE BENEDICTINE
1 OUNCE LEMON JUICE
1 TEASPOON SUGAR
CLUB SODA

Shake all ingredients except club soda well with cracked ice and strain into a tall glass that is half filled with ice cubes. Top off with club soda.
• Garnish with any of or all the following: lemon slice, orange slice, cherry.

CHRYSANTHEMUM

1¼ OUNCES DRY VERMOUTH
1¼ OUNCES BENEDICTINE
½ TEASPOON PERNOD

Shake all ingredients well with cracked ice and strain into a chilled cocktail glass.
• Add a twist of orange or lemon peel.

CREME DE MENTHE FRAPPE

GREEN CREME DE MENTHE

Fill a cocktail glass with crushed ice and add crème de menthe.

GOLD CADILLAC

¾ OUNCE GALLIANO
¾ OUNCE CREME DE CACAO
¾ OUNCE CREAM

Shake all ingredients well with cracked ice and strain into a chilled cocktail glass.

GRASSHOPPER

¾ OUNCE GREEN CREME
DE MENTHE
¾ OUNCE CREME DE CACAO
¾ OUNCE CREAM

Shake all ingredients well with cracked ice and strain into chilled cocktail glass.

MOCHA MINT

¾ OUNCE CREME DE MENTHE
¾ OUNCE CREME DE CACAO
¾ OUNCE KAHLUA *OR*
TIA MARIA

Shake all ingredients well with cracked ice and strain into chilled cocktail glass.

POUSSE-CAFE

Pousse-cafés are after-dinner drinks made from cordials that have been layered to achieve a rainbow effect. Pour the liqueurs carefully over the back of a spoon into a pousse-café glass. The density of a given liqueur may vary from brand to brand; if you should have a failure, either change brands or change the order of the liqueurs. If you're serving pousse-cafés to guests, make them ahead of time and refrigerate. Here are some of the most popular combinations:

- CREME DE CACAO, BRANDY, CREAM
- COINTREAU, SWEDISH PUNCH, CREME DE CASSIS
- GRENADINE, HEAVY CREAM, CREME DE VIOLETTE
- CREME DE CACAO, CREME D'YVETTE, BRANDY, CREAM
- GRENADINE, CREME DE CACAO, DRAMBUIE, CREAM
- GRENADINE, MARASCHINO LIQUEUR, GREEN CREME DE MENTHE, CREME DE VIOLETTE, YELLOW CHARTREUSE, BRANDY

For all the above, pour in equal amounts in the order given.

SCARLETT O'HARA

1¼ OUNCES SOUTHERN COMFORT
1¼ OUNCES CRANBERRY JUICE
2 TEASPOONS LIME JUICE

Shake all ingredients well with cracked ice and strain into a chilled cocktail glass.

SLOE GIN FIZZ

2 OUNCES SLOE GIN
1 OUNCE LEMON JUICE
½ TEASPOON SUGAR
CLUB SODA

Shake all ingredients except club soda with cracked ice and strain into a highball glass that is half filled with ice cubes. Top off with club soda; stir.

SOUTHERN PEACH

¾ OUNCE SOUTHERN COMFORT
¾ OUNCE PEACH LIQUEUR
¾ OUNCE CREAM

Shake all ingredients well with cracked ice and strain into a chilled cocktail glass.
● Garnish with a slice of peach or a sprig of mint.

WHITE RUSSIAN

¾ OUNCE VODKA
¾ OUNCE KAHLUA *OR* TIA MARIA
¾ OUNCE CREAM

Shake all ingredients well with cracked ice and strain into a chilled cocktail glass.
● The cream can be floated on the vodka and Kahlúa mixture.

Gin Cocktails

ABBEY

1½ OUNCES GIN
1 OUNCE ORANGE JUICE
DASH ORANGE BITTERS

Shake all ingredients well with cracked ice and strain into a chilled cocktail glass.

ALEXANDER

¾ OUNCE GIN
¾ OUNCE CREME DE CACAO
¾ OUNCE CREAM

Shake all ingredients well with cracked ice and strain into a chilled cocktail glass.

ALEXANDER'S SISTER

¾ OUNCE GIN
¾ OUNCE CREME DE MENTHE
¾ OUNCE CREAM

Shake well with ice and strain into chilled cocktail glass.

BELMONT

1½ OUNCES GIN
1 TEASPOON RASPBERRY
SYRUP *OR* GRENADINE
¾ OUNCE CREAM

Shake all ingredients well with cracked ice and strain into a chilled cocktail glass.

BENNETT

1½ OUNCES GIN
1 TABLESPOON LIME JUICE
½ TEASPOON SUGAR
2 DASHES ANGOSTURA
BITTERS

Shake all ingredients well with cracked ice. Strain into a chilled cocktail glass.
• Garnish with a twist of lime peel.

BRONX

1 OUNCE GIN
½ OUNCE DRY VERMOUTH
½ OUNCE SWEET VERMOUTH
1 TABLESPOON
ORANGE JUICE

Shake all ingredients well with cracked ice and strain into a chilled cocktail glass.

CLOVER CLUB

1½ OUNCES GIN
1 TABLESPOON LEMON JUICE
2 TEASPOONS GRENADINE
1 EGG WHITE

Shake all ingredients well with cracked ice and strain into chilled cocktail glass.

CLUB

1½ OUNCES GIN
¾ OUNCE SWEET VERMOUTH

Stir both ingredients well with ice and strain into a chilled cocktail glass.
- Garnish with an olive or a cherry.
- For a different flavor, try adding a dash of yellow Chartreuse.

GIMLET

1 OUNCE GIN
1 OUNCE LIME JUICE

Stir gin and lime juice well with ice and strain into chilled cocktail glass.
- Frost the rim of the glass by moistening with lime juice and dipping in sugar.
- Both fresh lime juice and Rose's Lime Juice are used in making gimlets.
- Vary proportions to suit personal taste. Gimlets may be made in any ratio from 1 to 1, as above, to 5 to 1.

GIN AND TONIC

2 OUNCES GIN
LIME WEDGE
QUININE WATER

Pour gin over cubes in a highball glass; squeeze lime and drop in. Top off with quinine water; stir.

GIN RICKEY

1½ OUNCES GIN
LIME WEDGE
CLUB SODA

Place ice cubes in a highball glass and pour in gin. Squeeze lime wedge over glass and drop in. Top off with club soda; stir.

MARTINI

2 OUNCES GIN

Pour gin over very cold cracked ice in a mixing glass or pitcher; then, depending on how "dry" you want your martini, add one of the following:

1 TEASPOON DRY VERMOUTH (12 to 1)

1½ TEASPOONS DRY VERMOUTH (9 to 1)

2 TEASPOONS DRY VERMOUTH (6 to 1)

1 TABLESPOON DRY VERMOUTH (4 to 1)

1 OUNCE DRY VERMOUTH (2 to 1)

Stir very well and strain into a well-chilled cocktail glass or over rocks in an old-fashioned glass. Garnish with an olive, stuffed or unstuffed, or a twist of lemon peel. When garnished with a cocktail onion, a martini becomes a gibson.

• The 12 to 1 martini is the driest, the 2 to 1, the least dry.

PERFECT

1½ OUNCES GIN
½ OUNCE DRY VERMOUTH
½ OUNCE SWEET VERMOUTH
DASH ANGOSTURA BITTERS
(OPTIONAL)

Stir all ingredients well with cracked ice and strain into a chilled cocktail glass.

● Garnish with olive or twist of lemon peel.

PINK LADY

1½ OUNCES GIN
1 TEASPOON GRENADINE
1 TEASPOON LIME JUICE
1 TEASPOON CREAM
1 EGG WHITE

Shake all ingredients well with cracked ice and strain into a chilled cocktail glass.

● Rim glass with sugar by moistening with lime juice and dipping into sugar.

PRINCETON

1½ OUNCES GIN
¾ OUNCE DRY VERMOUTH
1 TABLESPOON LIME JUICE

Stir all ingredients well with ice and strain into a chilled cocktail glass.

RAMOS FIZZ

2 OUNCES GIN
1 EGG WHITE
1 TABLESPOON CREAM
1 TABLESPOON LEMON JUICE
1 TABLESPOON LIME JUICE
1 TEASPOON SUGAR
3 DASHES ORANGE-FLOWER WATER
1 CUP CRACKED ICE
CLUB SODA

Place all ingredients except club soda into blender; cover and blend at high speed 5 to 7 seconds. Pour into tall glass and top off with club soda.

SINGAPORE SLING

2 OUNCES GIN
1 OUNCE CHERRY BRANDY
1 OUNCE LEMON
OR LIME JUICE
CLUB SODA

Shake all ingredients except club soda with cracked ice. Strain into a tall glass that is half filled with ice cubes. Top off with club soda.
● **Garnish with a slice of lemon or lime.**

TOM COLLINS

2 OUNCES GIN
1 OUNCE LEMON JUICE
1 TEASPOON SUGAR
CLUB SODA

Shake all ingredients except club soda with cracked ice and strain into a collins glass that is half filled with ice cubes. Top off with club soda.
● **Garnish with any of or all the following: lemon slice, orange slice, maraschino cherry.**
● **To make a john collins, use Hollands, geneva, or Schiedam gin.**

73

WHITE ROSE

1 OUNCE GIN
1 TABLESPOON LEMON JUICE
1 TABLESPOON LIME JUICE
1 TEASPOON SUGAR
1 EGG WHITE

Shake all ingredients well with cracked ice and strain into a chilled cocktail glass.

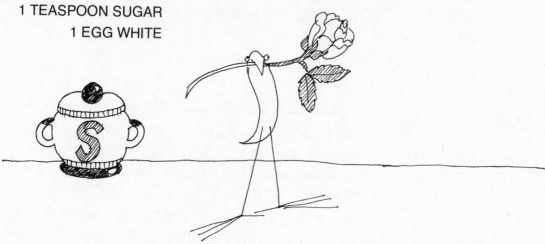

Irish-Whiskey Cocktails

IRISH COFFEE

1½ OUNCES IRISH WHISKEY
4 to 6 OUNCES HOT
BLACK COFFEE
1 TEASPOON SUGAR
1 TABLESPOON SWEETENED
WHIPPED CREAM

Put whiskey, coffee, and 1 teaspoon sugar into a warmed Irish coffee glass, coffee cup, or mug. Stir to dissolve sugar. Top with whipped cream.

IRISH COOLER

2 OUNCES IRISH WHISKEY
1 TEASPOON CREME
DE MENTHE
CLUB SODA

Place ice in a highball glass. Pour in whiskey and crème de menthe. Top off with club soda.
• Add a twist of lemon peel or a sprig of mint.

IRISH FIX

1 TABLESPOON LEMON JUICE
1 TEASPOON SUGAR
1½ OUNCES IRISH WHISKEY
1 TABLESPOON IRISH MIST

Put lemon juice and sugar into a highball glass and stir until sugar is dissolved. Fill glass with crushed ice. Pour in Irish whiskey and stir. Add crushed ice to fill. Float Irish Mist on top.
• Garnish with orange slice, lemon slice, or sprig of mint dipped in confectioners sugar.

PADDY

1¼ OUNCES IRISH WHISKEY
1¼ OUNCES SWEET
VERMOUTH
DASH ANGOSTURA BITTERS

Shake all ingredients well with cracked ice and strain into a chilled cocktail glass.

ST. PATRICK'S DAY

1 OUNCE IRISH WHISKEY
1 OUNCE GREEN CREME DE MENTHE
¾ OUNCE GREEN CHARTREUSE

Shake all ingredients well with cracked ice and strain into a chilled cocktail glass.

SHILLELAGH

1½ OUNCES IRISH WHISKEY
½ OUNCE SLOE GIN
½ OUNCE LIGHT RUM
1 TABLESPOON LEMON JUICE
1 TEASPOON SUGAR

Shake all ingredients well with cracked ice and strain into a chilled old-fashioned glass.
• Garnish with any of or all of the following: peach slice, strawberry, maraschino cherry, mint sprig.

Rum Cocktails

BACARDI

1½ OUNCES LIGHT RUM *OR*
BACARDI RUM
1 TABLESPOON LIME JUICE
1 TEASPOON GRENADINE

Shake well with cracked ice and strain into a chilled cocktail glass or over rocks in an old-fashioned glass.

BEACHCOMBER

1½ OUNCES LIGHT RUM
½ OUNCE TRIPLE SEC *OR*
COINTREAU
2 DASHES MARASCHINO
LIQUEUR
1 TABLESPOON LIME JUICE

Shake all ingredients well with cracked ice and strain into a chilled cocktail glass.
• Frost the glass with sugar by moistening the rim with lime juice and dipping it in sugar.

BOLERO

1½ OUNCES LIGHT RUM
¾ OUNCE APPLE BRANDY
¼ TEASPOON SWEET
VERMOUTH

Shake all ingredients well with cracked ice and strain into chilled cocktail glass.
● Garnish with twist of lemon peel.

BOLO

1½ OUNCES LIGHT RUM
1 TABLESPOON ORANGE
JUICE
1 TABLESPOON LEMON JUICE
OR LIME JUICE
½ TEASPOON SUGAR

Shake well with cracked ice and strain into a chilled cocktail glass or sour glass.
● Garnish with a lemon slice or orange slice.

CUBA LIBRE

1½ OUNCES LIGHT RUM
LIME WEDGE
COLA

Fill a highball or collins glass halfway with ice cubes. Pour in rum, squeeze juice from lime wedge and drop in, and fill with cola; stir.

CUBAN SPECIAL

1½ OUNCES LIGHT RUM
½ TEASPOON CURACAO
1 TABLESPOON PINEAPPLE
JUICE
1 TABLESPOON LIME *OR*
LEMON JUICE

Shake all ingredients well with cracked ice and strain into a chilled cocktail glass.
• Garnish with a chunk of pineapple and a cherry.

DAIQUIRI

1½ OUNCES LIGHT RUM
1 OUNCE LIME JUICE
1 TEASPOON SUGAR

**Shake well with ice and strain into a chilled cocktail glass or over rocks in an old-fashioned glass.
• Frost the glass with sugar by moistening the rim with lime juice and dipping it in sugar.**

EL PRESIDENTE

1½ OUNCES GOLDEN RUM
½ OUNCE CURACAO
½ OUNCE DRY VERMOUTH
2 DASHES GRENADINE

Shake all ingredients well with ice and strain into a chilled cocktail glass.

FROZEN DAIQUIRI

1½ OUNCES LIGHT RUM
1 OUNCE LIME JUICE
1 TEASPOON SUGAR
½ CUP CRUSHED ICE

Place all ingredients in blender. Cover and blend at low speed 7 to 12 seconds. Pour into a chilled saucer champagne glass.

HOT BUTTERED RUM I

1½ OUNCES LIGHT RUM
1 TABLESPOON BROWN
SUGAR
1 TEASPOON BUTTER
¼ TEASPOON GROUND
CLOVES
¼ TEASPOON GROUND
CINNAMON
BOILING WATER
NUTMEG (OPTIONAL)

Put rum, brown sugar, butter, cloves, and cinnamon in a mug or hot whiskey glass and fill with boiling water; stir. Top with grated nutmeg, if desired.
• In place of the ground cloves and cinnamon, use 2 or 3 whole cloves and a stick of cinnamon.

MAI TAI

2½ OUNCES LIGHT RUM
½ OUNCE TRIPLE SEC *OR* COINTREAU
2 TEASPOONS ORZATA, ORGEAT, *OR* ALMOND-FLAVORED SYRUP
2 TEASPOONS GRENADINE
1 TABLESPOON LIME JUICE
½ TEASPOON SUGAR

Shake well with ice and strain into a chilled double old-fashioned glass. Add crushed or cracked ice to fill.

● Garnish with any or all the following: pineapple stick, maraschino cherry, lime slice, sprig of mint.

NAVY GROG

1 OUNCE DARK RUM
1 OUNCE LIGHT RUM
1 TABLESPOON LIME JUICE
1 TABLESPOON ORANGE
JUICE
1 TABLESPOON GUAVA
NECTAR
2 TEASPOONS ORZATA,
ORGEAT, *OR*
ALMOND-FLAVORED SYRUP

Shake well with cracked ice and strain into chilled double old-fashioned glass. Add crushed ice to fill. • Garnish with mint sprig, lime slice, or orange slice.

PLANTER'S PUNCH

2 OUNCES DARK RUM
1 OUNCE LIME JUICE
1 TEASPOON SUGAR
DASH ANGOSTURA BITTERS

Shake well with cracked ice. Strain into a collins glass that is half filled with crushed ice; add crushed ice to fill.

• Garnish with any of or all the following: lemon, lime, or orange slice; pineapple stick, maraschino cherry, mint sprig.

RUM DUBONNET

1½ OUNCES LIGHT RUM
1 OUNCE RED DUBONNET
1 LIME WEDGE

Shake rum and Dubonnet well with cracked ice and strain into a chilled cocktail glass. Squeeze juice from lime wedge into drink and drop in the wedge; stir.

RUM EGGNOG

2 OUNCES LIGHT RUM
1 EGG
1 TEASPOON SUGAR
4 OUNCES MILK
NUTMEG

Shake all ingredients except nutmeg well with cracked ice and strain into a collins or highball glass. Top with grated nutmeg, if desired.

SCORPION

1½ OUNCES LIGHT RUM
1 OUNCE BRANDY
1½ OUNCES LEMON JUICE
1½ OUNCES ORANGE JUICE
1 TABLESPOON ORZATA,
ORGEAT, *OR*
ALMOND-FLAVORED SYRUP

Shake well with cracked ice and strain into a chilled double old-fashioned glass. Add crushed ice to fill.
• Garnish with a sprig of mint, an orange slice, or a few rose petals.

SEPTEMBER MORN

1½ OUNCES LIGHT RUM
1 TABLESPOON LIME JUICE
1 TEASPOON GRENADINE
1 EGG WHITE

Shake all ingredients well with cracked ice and strain into a chilled cocktail glass.
● Frost the glass by moistening the rim with lime juice and dipping it in sugar.

ZOMBIE

1½ OUNCES GOLDEN RUM
1 OUNCE DARK RUM
1 OUNCE LIGHT RUM
1 OUNCE PINEAPPLE JUICE
1 OUNCE LIME JUICE
1 TEASPOON GRENADINE
½ TEASPOON SUGAR
1 TEASPOON 151-PROOF
DEMERARA RUM (OPTIONAL)

Shake well with cracked ice and strain into a chilled 14-ounce glass. Add crushed ice to fill. Float 151-proof rum on top, if desired.
● Garnish with any of or all the following: pineapple chunk, maraschino cherry, lime slice, mint sprig. Sprinkle with confectioners sugar and serve with straws.

89

BOBBY BURNS

1¼ OUNCES SCOTCH
1¼ OUNCES SWEET
VERMOUTH
1 TEASPOON BENEDICTINE
LEMON PEEL

Shake well with ice and strain into a chilled cocktail glass. Twist lemon peel over drink and drop in.

HOLE IN ONE

2 OUNCES SCOTCH
¾ OUNCE DRY VERMOUTH
2 DASHES LEMON JUICE
DASH ORANGE BITTERS

Shake all ingredients well with ice and strain into a chilled cocktail glass.
● Add a twist of lemon or orange peel.

ROB ROY

2 OUNCES SCOTCH
¾ OUNCE SWEET VERMOUTH
DASH ORANGE BITTERS

Shake all ingredients well with cracked ice and strain into a chilled cocktail glass.

ROB ROY, DRY

2 OUNCES SCOTCH
¾ OUNCE DRY VERMOUTH
DASH ANGOSTURA BITTERS

Shake all ingredients well with cracked ice and strain into a chilled cocktail glass.

RUSTY NAIL

1 OUNCE SCOTCH
¾ OUNCE DRAMBUIE

Pour over rocks in a chilled old-fashioned glass and stir.

SCOTCH BISHOP

1½ OUNCES SCOTCH
½ OUNCE DRY VERMOUTH
3 DASHES TRIPLE SEC
1 TABLESPOON ORANGE
JUICE

Shake all ingredients well with cracked ice and strain into a chilled cocktail glass.
• Add a twist of lemon peel.

SCOTCH COOLER

2 OUNCES SCOTCH
1 TEASPOON CREME
DE MENTHE
CLUB SODA

Stir Scotch and crème de menthe in a highball glass. Fill with ice cubes and add club soda.

SCOTCH MILK PUNCH

2 OUNCES SCOTCH
6 OUNCES MILK
1 TEASPOON SUGAR
NUTMEG (OPTIONAL)

Shake all ingredients except nutmeg well with cracked ice and strain into a chilled collins glass. Top with grated nutmeg, if desired.

SCOTCH MIST

CRUSHED ICE
SCOTCH
LEMON PEEL

Fill an old-fashioned glass with crushed ice. Add Scotch to taste. Twist lemon peel over drink and drop in.

SCOTCH SOUR

2 OUNCES SCOTCH
1 TABLESPOON LEMON JUICE
1 TEASPOON LIME JUICE
1 TEASPOON SUGAR

Shake all ingredients well with cracked ice and strain into a chilled sour glass.
● Garnish with any of or all the following: lemon slice, orange slice, lime slice, maraschino cherry.

STONE FENCE

2 OUNCES SCOTCH
2 DASHES ANGOSTURA
BITTERS
CLUB SODA

Fill a highball glass with ice cubes. Add Scotch and bitters; top off with club soda.
● Decorate with a slice of lemon, orange, or lime.

Tequila Cocktails

BLOODY MARIA

1½ OUNCES TEQUILA
3 OUNCES TOMATO JUICE
1 TEASPOON LEMON JUICE
DASH TABASCO SAUCE
SALT AND PEPPER

Shake well with cracked ice and strain into a chilled highball glass or over rocks in an old-fashioned glass.
- Add a dash or two of Worcestershire sauce, if desired.
- Garnish with a celery stalk and a slice of lemon.

FROZEN MATADOR

1½ OUNCES TEQUILA
1½ OUNCES PINEAPPLE JUICE
1 TABLESPOON LIME JUICE

Place all ingredients, along with about ¾ cup cracked ice, in a blender. Blend at medium speed 7 to 12 seconds. Pour into chilled old-fashioned glass. Add crushed ice to fill.
- Garnish with a lime slice and/or a pineapple stick.

FROZEN MEXICAN BLACKBERRY

1½ OUNCES TEQUILA
1 OUNCE BLACKBERRY
LIQUEUR
1 TABLESPOON LIME JUICE
½ TEASPOON SUGAR

Place all ingredients, along with about ¾ cup cracked ice, in a blender. Blend at medium speed 7 to 12 seconds. Pour into a chilled old-fashioned glass. Add crushed ice to fill.
● Garnish with lime or lemon slice.

MARGARITA

1½ OUNCES TEQUILA
½ OUNCE TRIPLE SEC
OR COINTREAU
¾ OUNCE LEMON OR LIME
JUICE

Moisten the rim of a cocktail glass with lemon or lime juice and dip into salt. Shake ingredients well with cracked ice and strain into glass.
● You may prefer to make this drink in a blender: Add cracked ice and blend at medium speed 5 to 7 seconds; pour into glass. This method makes a "semifrozen" margarita.

SUNRISE

---

3 DASHES GRENADINE
1½ OUNCES TEQUILA
ORANGE JUICE

Put grenadine into a highball glass. Add ice cubes and pour in tequila. Add orange juice to fill.
• The sunrise effect is achieved by leaving the drink unstirred. You may, however, prefer to stir before imbibing.

SUNSET

1½ OUNCES TEQUILA
1 TABLESPOON GRENADINE
1 TABLESPOON LIME JUICE

Place all ingredients, along with about 1 cup of cracked ice, in a blender. Blend at medium speed 7 to 12 seconds. Pour into a chilled old-fashioned glass and add crushed ice to fill, if necessary.

TEQUILA DUBONNET

1¼ OUNCES TEQUILA
1¼ OUNCES RED DUBONNET

Shake well with cracked ice and strain into chilled cocktail glass or over rocks in an old-fashioned glass.
• Add a twist of lemon peel.

TEQUILA OLD FASHIONED

1 TEASPOON WATER
DASH ANGOSTURA BITTERS
½ TEASPOON SUGAR
1½ OUNCES TEQUILA

Put water, bitters, and sugar into an old-fashioned glass and stir until sugar is dissolved. Fill glass with cracked ice and pour in tequila; stir well.
• Add a twist of lemon peel, or garnish with a lemon or lime slice.

TEQUINI

2 OUNCES TEQUILA
½ OUNCE DRY VERMOUTH

Stir tequila and vermouth well with cracked ice and strain into a chilled cocktail glass.
- Add a twist of lemon peel.
- For variations, see gin martini, page 70, and substitute tequila for gin.

TEQUONIC

1½ OUNCES TEQUILA
1 TABLESPOON LEMON
OR LIME JUICE
QUININE WATER

Fill an old-fashioned glass with cracked ice. Add tequila, fruit juice, and quinine water; stir well.

Vodka Cocktails

BLACK MAGIC (RUSSIAN ESPRESSO)

1½ OUNCES VODKA
¾ OUNCE ESPRESSO
LIQUEUR
1 TABLESPOON LEMON JUICE
LEMON PEEL

Add ice cubes to a chilled old-fashioned glass. Pour in vodka, espresso liqueur, and lemon juice. Stir well; twist lemon peel over glass and add.
● **Try adding a dash or two of Pernod.**

BLACK RUSSIAN

1½ OUNCES VODKA
¾ OUNCE KAHLUA LIQUEUR

Either shake the vodka and Kahlúa well with ice and strain into a cube-filled, chilled old-fashioned glass, or simply pour ingredients over rocks in a chilled old-fashioned glass and stir well.

BLOODY MARY

1½ OUNCES VODKA
3 OUNCES TOMATO JUICE
1 TEASPOON LEMON JUICE
DASH TABASCO SAUCE
SALT AND PEPPER

Shake all ingredients well with cracked ice and strain into glass.
• Add a dash or two of Worcestershire sauce, if desired.
• Garnish with a celery stalk and a lemon slice.

BULL SHOT

1½ OUNCES VODKA
3 OUNCES CHILLED
BEEF BOUILLON
DASH WORCESTERSHIRE
SAUCE
SALT AND PEPPER

Shake all ingredients well with cracked ice and strain into an old-fashioned glass.

CAPE CODDER

1½ OUNCES VODKA
3 OUNCES CRANBERRY JUICE
½ TEASPOON LIME JUICE

Shake well with ice and strain into a cube-filled old-fashioned glass.
- Try serving in a highball glass and topping off with club soda.
- A sprig of fresh mint makes an excellent garnish.

FLYING GRASSHOPPER (VODKA GRASSHOPPER)

1 OUNCE VODKA
1 OUNCE GREEN CREME DE MENTHE
1 OUNCE WHITE CREME DE CACAO

Stir well with cracked ice. Strain into a chilled cocktail glass.

HARVEY WALLBANGER

1 OUNCE VODKA
½ OUNCE GALLIANO
3 OUNCES ORANGE JUICE

Shake well with cracked ice and strain into a large cocktail glass or over rocks in a tall glass.

KRETCHMA

1 OUNCE VODKA
1 OUNCE CREME DE CACAO
1 TABLESPOON LEMON JUICE
DASH GRENADINE

Shake well with ice and strain into a chilled cocktail glass.

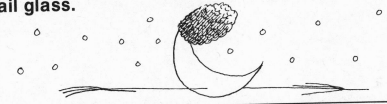

MOSCOW MULE

1½ OUNCES VODKA
½ LIME
6 OUNCES GINGER ALE

Place ice cubes in a large glass or mug and pour vodka over. Squeeze juice from lime and drop rind into glass. Top off with ginger ale; stir well.

RUSSIAN BEAR

1½ OUNCES VODKA
½ OUNCE CREME DE CACAO
½ OUNCE CREAM

Shake all ingredients well with cracked ice and strain into a chilled cocktail glass.

SALTY DOG

1½ OUNCES VODKA
3 OUNCES GRAPEFRUIT JUICE
SALT

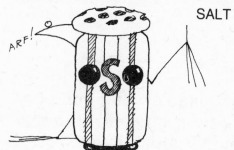

Shake all ingredients well with ice and strain into a large cocktail glass or over rocks in an old-fashioned glass.
• Before pouring the drink, frost the glass with salt by moistening the rim with lemon juice and dipping it in salt.
• This drink is sometimes made with gin instead of vodka.

106

SCREWDRIVER

1½ OUNCES VODKA
3 OUNCES ORANGE JUICE

Shake well with cracked ice and strain into a large cocktail glass or over rocks in an old-fashioned glass.
• Garnish with a slice of lemon or orange and a maraschino cherry.

TOVARICH

1½ OUNCES VODKA
¾ OUNCE KUMMEL
1 TABLESPOON LIME JUICE

Shake all ingredients well with cracked ice and strain into a chilled cocktail glass.
• Add a twist of lime peel.

VODKA COLLINS

2 OUNCES VODKA
1 TABLESPOON LEMON JUICE
1 TEASPOON SUGAR
CLUB SODA

Shake all ingredients except club soda well with cracked ice and strain into a chilled collins glass that is half filled with ice. Fill with club soda; stir.
● Garnish with any of or all the following: lemon slice, orange slice, maraschino cherry.

VODKA DAISY

2 OUNCES VODKA
2 TABLESPOONS LIME JUICE
1 TEASPOON GRENADINE
½ TEASPOON SUGAR

Shake all ingredients well with cracked ice and strain into a tall glass or stein. Add cracked ice to fill.
● Garnish with a lime slice, a lemon slice, or a maraschino cherry.

VODKA GIMLET

1½ OUNCES VODKA
1 TABLESPOON LIME JUICE
OR ROSE'S LIME JUICE
1 TEASPOON SUGAR

Stir all ingredients well with cracked ice and strain into a chilled cocktail glass.

VODKA GYPSY

1½ OUNCES VODKA
1 OUNCE BENEDICTINE
DASH ANGOSTURA BITTERS

Stir all ingredients well with cracked ice and strain into a chilled cocktail glass.

VODKA MARTINI

See gin martini, page 70, and substitute vodka for gin.

Whiskey Cocktails

BLACK HAWK

1¼ OUNCES WHISKEY
1¼ OUNCES SLOE GIN
1 TEASPOON LEMON JUICE

Shake all ingredients well with cracked ice and strain into a chilled cocktail glass.
● Garnish with a lemon slice and/or a maraschino cherry.

COMMODORE

1½ OUNCES WHISKEY
1 TABLESPOON LEMON *OR* LIME JUICE
2 DASHES ORANGE BITTERS

Shake all ingredients well with cracked ice and strain into a chilled cocktail glass.

EARTHQUAKE

¾ OUNCE WHISKEY
¾ OUNCE GIN
¾ OUNCE PERNOD

Shake all ingredients well with cracked ice and strain into a chilled cocktail glass.

LOS ANGELES

1½ OUNCES WHISKEY
¼ TEASPOON SWEET
VERMOUTH
1 TABLESPOON LEMON JUICE
1 TEASPOON SUGAR
1 EGG

Shake all ingredients well with ice and strain into a chilled old-fashioned glass. Add cracked ice, if you wish.

MANHATTAN

2 OUNCES WHISKEY
½ TO 1 OUNCE SWEET
VERMOUTH
DASH ANGOSTURA BITTERS
(OPTIONAL)

Stir all ingredients well with cracked ice and strain into a chilled cocktail glass.
• Garnish with a maraschino cherry.
• For a more mellow manhattan, add ¼ teaspoon maraschino cherry juice.
• To make a dry manhattan, substitute dry vermouth for the sweet and garnish with twist of lemon peel or an olive.

MILK PUNCH

1½ OUNCES WHISKEY
4 OUNCES MILK
1 TEASPOON SUGAR

Shake all ingredients well with cracked ice and strain into a chilled collins glass.
- **Top with grated nutmeg, if desired.**

MINT JULEP

4 SPRIGS FRESH MINT
1 TEASPOON WATER
1 TEASPOON SUGAR
2 OUNCES BOURBON

Tear leaves on 2 of the sprigs of mint and place in a collins glass or silver mug along with water and sugar; muddle until sugar is dissolved. Fill glass with finely cracked ice and pour in bourbon. Stir until glass is frosted. Add more cracked ice to fill and decorate with remaining 2 sprigs of mint. Serve with straws, if you wish.

NEW YORK

1½ OUNCES WHISKEY
1 TABLESPOON LEMON *OR*
LIME JUICE
½ TEASPOON GRENADINE
1 TEASPOON SUGAR

Shake all ingredients well with cracked ice and strain into a chilled cocktail glass.
● Add a twist of orange and/or lemon peel.

NEW YORK SOUR

2 OUNCES WHISKEY
1 OUNCE DRY RED WINE
1 TABLESPOON LEMON JUICE
1 TEASPOON SUGAR

Shake all ingredients well with cracked ice and strain into a chilled sour glass.
● Garnish with a slice of lemon.

OLD FASHIONED

1 TEASPOON WATER
½ TEASPOON SUGAR
2 DASHES ANGOSTURA
BITTERS
1½ OUNCES WHISKEY

In a chilled old-fashioned glass, stir water, sugar, and bitters until the sugar is dissolved. Fill glass with cracked ice and pour in whiskey; stir well.
● Garnish with any of or all the following: orange slice, lemon slice, maraschino cherry.
● Virtually any liquor can be substituted for the whiskey in this recipe.

SAZERAC

2 OUNCES BOURBON *OR*
BLENDED WHISKEY
½ TEASPOON PERNOD
½ TEASPOON SUGAR
2 DASHES PEYCHAUD'S *OR*
ANGOSTURA BITTERS

Stir all ingredients well with ice and strain into a chilled cocktail glass or over rocks in an old-fashioned glass.
● The sazerac is a delightful brunch or mid-afternoon drink.

WARD EIGHT

2 OUNCES WHISKEY
1 TABLESPOON LEMON JUICE
1 TEASPOON GRENADINE
1 TEASPOON SUGAR

Shake all ingredients well with cracked ice and strain into a highball glass that is half filled with ice cubes.
● Garnish with any of or all the following: lemon slice, orange slice, maraschino cherry.

WHISKEY SOUR

2 OUNCES WHISKEY
1 TABLESPOON LEMON JUICE
1 TEASPOON SUGAR

Shake all ingredients well with cracked ice and strain into a chilled sour glass.
● Garnish with any of or all the following: lemon slice, orange slice, maraschino cherry.
● Virtually any liquor can be substituted for the whiskey in this recipe.

WHISKEY SOUR II

1½ OUNCES WHISKEY
1 TABLESPOON LEMON JUICE
1 TABLESPOON ORANGE
JUICE
1 TEASPOON SUGAR

Shake all ingredients well with cracked ice and strain into a chilled sour glass.
- **Garnish with a cherry, an orange slice, or a lemon slice.**
- **As in the regular whiskey sour recipe, you can substitute almost any liquor for the whiskey.**

WHISKEY TODDY (HOT)

1 TEASPOON SUGAR
BOILING WATER
2 OUNCES WHISKEY
NUTMEG (OPTIONAL)

Put sugar in a hot whiskey glass, coffee cup, or mug and fill about ⅔ full with boiling water. Add whiskey and stir. Top with grated nutmeg, if desired.
- **Decorate with a slice of lemon.**

117

Nonalcoholic Cocktails

ALHAMBRA

1 OUNCE GRENADINE
GINGER ALE

Place ice cubes in an old-fashioned glass and pour in grenadine. Add ginger ale to fill.
• Garnish with a maraschino cherry and an orange slice.

BANANA FRAPPE

½ RIPE BANANA
4 OUNCES MILK
1 SCOOP VANILLA ICE CREAM
¼ TEASPOON VANILLA
EXTRACT
1 TABLESPOON HONEY
NUTMEG

Place all ingredients except nutmeg in a blender and blend at medium speed 10 to 15 seconds. Top with grated nutmeg.
• Substitute a handful of strawberries, red raspberries, or ripe peach wedges for the banana.

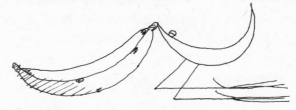

119

CLAMATO COCKTAIL

4 OUNCES CHILLED
CLAM JUICE
4 OUNCES TOMATO JUICE
1 TEASPOON LEMON JUICE
DASH TABASCO SAUCE
PINCH CELERY SALT
SALT AND PEPPER

Shake all ingredients well with cracked ice and strain into a tall glass. Add ice cubes, if you wish.
• Add a jigger of vodka to this, if you wish.

COFFEE EGGNOG

1 EGG, SEPARATED
3 OUNCES STRONG,
COLD COFFEE
3 OUNCES CREAM
¼ TEASPOON VANILLA EXTRACT
1 TABLESPOON SUGAR
NUTMEG (OPTIONAL)

Beat egg yolk until lemon-colored; stir in coffee, cream, and vanilla. Beat egg white until stiff, adding sugar a little at a time. Fold egg white gently into egg-yolk mixture. Pour into a tall glass and top with grated nutmeg, if desired.

CRANBERRY GLOGG

3 OUNCES CRANBERRY JUICE
3 OUNCES APPLE CIDER
1 TEASPOON GRATED
ORANGE PEEL
1 TEASPOON BLANCHED
ALMONDS
2 CLOVES
CINNAMON STICK,
½ INCH LONG
2 TEASPOONS RAISINS

Place all ingredients in a saucepan and heat gently for 5 minutes. Strain liquid into a hot whiskey glass, coffee cup, or mug, adding a few raisins and almonds to the drink.

HAWAIIAN DELIGHT

⅔ CUP CRUSHED PINEAPPLE
1 CARROT, CUT UP
1 SLICE BANANA,
2 INCHES THICK
2 TEASPOONS HONEY
1 TEASPOON UNSWEETENED
GRATED COCONUT

Place all ingredients in a blender with cracked ice and blend at medium speed 10 to 15 seconds, or until smooth. Serve in a tall glass.

NANTUCKET FLOAT

4 OUNCES CHILLED
CRANBERRY JUICE
4 OUNCES CHILLED
PINEAPPLE JUICE
1 SCOOP LIME SHERBET

Combine the juices in a tall glass and top with the sherbet.
• Garnish with a lime slice and a mint sprig.

PARISETTE

1 TABLESPOON GRENADINE	**Place several ice cubes in a highball glass. Add**
4 OUNCES MILK	**grenadine and milk and stir.**

PIKE'S PEAK COOLER

1 TABLESPOON LEMON JUICE	**Shake all ingredients except apple juice with**
1 EGG	**cracked ice and strain into a tall glass. Fill with ap-**
1 TEASPOON SUGAR	**ple juice and stir.**
APPLE JUICE	**• Use hard cider instead of apple juice, if you**
	wish.

PINK PEARL

1½ OUNCES GRAPEFRUIT JUICE 1 TEASPOON GRENADINE ¼ TEASPOON LEMON JUICE ½ EGG WHITE	Shake all ingredients well with cracked ice and strain into a chilled cocktail glass.

ROSEY SQUASH

1 OUNCE GRENADINE 2 TABLESPOONS LEMON JUICE CLUB SODA	Place several ice cubes in a highball glass. Add grenadine and lemon juice and fill with club soda; stir. ● Garnish with a lemon slice and a maraschino cherry.

SARATOGA II

1 TABLESPOON LEMON JUICE
½ TEASPOON SUGAR
DASH ANGOSTURA BITTERS
GINGER ALE

Place lemon juice and sugar in a highball glass and stir until sugar is dissolved. Add several ice cubes and fill with ginger ale.
● Garnish with a lemon slice.

SUMMER DAWN

1 OUNCE RASPBERRY SYRUP
2 TABLESPOONS LIME JUICE
CLUB SODA

Fill a tall glass halfway with cracked ice. Add raspberry syrup and lime juice and fill with club soda; stir.
● Garnish with a lime slice and a maraschino cherry.

PUNCHES

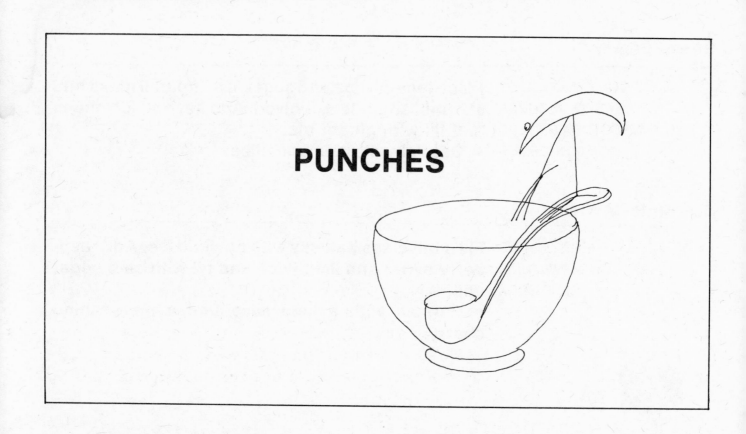

DECORATIVE ICE WREATH

To make a decorative ice wreath for your punch bowl, pour about 1 inch of water into a ring mold and freeze it. Arrange flowers—preferably edible ones, such as daisies, hibiscus flowers, chrysanthemums, roses, and squash blossoms—perfect, unhulled berries, citrus slices, cherries, or unpeeled fruit wedges in combination with fresh leaves cut from herb plants upside down on the ice. Add enough water to freeze the flowers, fruit, or leaves in place and return the mold to the freezer. When frozen, remove it from the freezer and fill the mold to the top with more water; freeze again until hard. Remove the wreath from the ring mold by running warm water over the bottom; keep in a plastic bag in the freezer until party time.

ALOHA

1 TABLESPOON FINELY
CHOPPED GINGER ROOT
2 CUPS SUGAR
2 CUPS WATER
2 CUPS CHILLED GUAVA JUICE
4 CUPS CRUSHED PINEAPPLE
1 CUP CHILLED APRICOT
NECTAR
3 CUPS CHILLED ORANGE
JUICE
½ CUP CHILLED LEMON JUICE
½ CUP CHILLED LIME JUICE
2 QUARTS CHILLED JAMAICA
RUM
FRESH MINT LEAVES

Combine the ginger root and sugar with the water in a pan and bring it to a boil. Simmer for about 15 minutes, stirring to dissolve the sugar. Strain out the ginger root and discard. Allow the liquid to cool. Combine with the remaining ingredients in a punch bowl over a block or ring of ice and garnish with mint. Serve in glasses with ice.

APRICOT-GIN FREEZE

about 20 servings

2 QUARTS LEMON SHERBET
4 CUPS APRICOT NECTAR
2 CUPS ORANGE JUICE
1 FIFTH GIN
THIN LEMON SLICES
MINT SPRIGS

In a large bowl, beat part of the lemon sherbet into the apricot nectar and orange juice till smooth. Add more sherbet and some of the gin and beat until smooth. Continue adding sherbet and gin until completely blended. Pour into a punch bowl and garnish with lemon slices and mint sprigs. Serve in tall, wide-mouthed glasses.

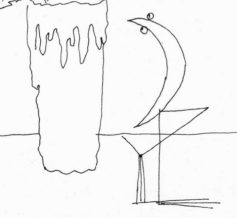

APRIL AMBROSIA

about 35 ½-cup servings

1 PINEAPPLE
1 FIFTH CHILLED ROSE
1 FIFTH CHILLED JAMAICA RUM
1 FIFTH CHILLED BOURBON
2 QUARTS CHILLED CHAMPAGNE
FRESH, UNHULLED STRAWBERRIES
LIME SLICES
MINT SPRIGS

Peel and thinly slice the pineapple; pour the rosé, rum, and bourbon over it and cover. Refrigerate for 24 hours. When ready to serve, place pineapple and liquor mixture in a punch bowl over a block or ring of ice and add champagne. Garnish with strawberries skewered with lime slices and mint sprigs. Serve in punch cups.

"BIG APPLE" FAVORITE   about 16 ½-cup servings

1 QUART GIN *OR* VODKA
1 QUART BITTER LEMON
THIN APPLE SLICES, UNPEELED

Pour ingredients over a block or ring of ice in a punch bowl and garnish with apple slices. Serve in punch cups.

BRANDIED FRENCH CHOCOLATE   about 6 servings

½ CUP SEMISWEET
CHOCOLATE BITS
¼ CUP WATER
1 QUART MILK
¼ CUP SUGAR
½ TEASPOON VANILLA
EXTRACT
¼ CUP BRANDY
SWEETENED WHIPPED CREAM
GRATED CHOCOLATE
(OPTIONAL)

Melt the chocolate in the water in a pan set over low heat, stirring constantly. In another pan, bring the milk just to the boiling point and then mix with the melted chocolate, sugar, vanilla, and brandy. Heat gently but do not boil. Pour into mugs and top with dollops of whipped cream . Sprinkle with grated chocolate if desired.

BURGUNDY COOLER   about 12 servings

¼ CUP WHISKEY
2 TABLESPOONS CURACAO
2 TABLESPOONS BENEDICTINE
2 FIFTHS CHILLED RED
BURGUNDY
½ CUP CHILLED ORANGE
JUICE
3 CUPS CHILLED CLUB SODA
½ CUP SUGAR
ORANGE SLICES
LIME SLICES
MINT SPRIGS

Place all ingredients except the orange and lime slices and mint sprigs in a large glass pitcher filled with ice cubes and stir gently to mix. Garnish the punch with the citrus slices cut in half and with fresh mint sprigs. Serve in tall glasses with ice.

CAFE BRULOT

about 8-10 servings

---

2 CINNAMON STICKS,
EACH 1 INCH LONG
10 CLOVES
1 THIN SLICE ORANGE
PEEL
1 THIN SLICE LEMON PEEL
4 WHOLE ALLSPICE
6 SUGAR CUBES
1 TEASPOON VANILLA
EXTRACT
1 CUP COGNAC
4 CUPS STRONG, HOT COFFEE

Heat all ingredients except the coffee in a chafing dish, stirring until all the sugar is dissolved. Then ignite the mixture and stir in the hot coffee, continuing to stir until the flame dies. Serve in demitasse cups.

CARIBBEAN DAZZLER   about 30 ½-cup servings

1 FIFTH CHILLED RED WINE
1 FIFTH CHILLED WHISKEY
2 CUPS CHILLED JAMAICA
RUM
2 TABLESPOONS BENEDICTINE
¾ CUP CHILLED
APRICOT BRANDY
¾ CUP CHILLED COINTREAU
3 CUPS CHILLED ORANGE
JUICE
2 CUPS CHILLED LEMON JUICE
ORANGE SLICES
LEMON SLICES
MINT SPRIGS

Combine all ingredients except the orange and lemon slices and mint sprigs in a punch bowl over a block or a ring of ice. Garnish with orange and lemon slices and mint sprigs and serve in punch cups.

CHABLIS COCKTAILS — about 8-10 servings

½ CUP BENEDICTINE
2 FIFTHS CHILLED CHABLIS
FRESH PINEAPPLE WEDGES
SMALL, WHOLE STRAWBERRIES

Mix the Benedictine with the wine in a large glass pitcher filled with ice. Garnish the pitcher with fresh pineapple wedges skewered with strawberries and serve in large white-wine glasses.

CHAMPAGNE FIZZER — about 14 ½-cup servings

4 SUGAR CUBES
ANGOSTURA BITTERS
¾ CUP BRANDY
2 FIFTHS CHILLED CHAMPAGNE
ORANGE SLICES (OPTIONAL)

Place sugar cubes in the bottom of a glass punch bowl and sprinkle them with the bitters. Add the brandy. Then add the champagne and a block or decorative ring of ice. Garnish with halved orange slices. Serve in champagne glasses.

135

CHILLED CAFE COGNAC   about 18 ½-cup servings

8 EGGS
¾ CUP SUGAR
4 CUPS STRONG COFFEE
1½ CUPS COGNAC
¼ TEASPOON NUTMEG
ORANGE SLICES

Beat eggs until thick and lemon in color. Continuing to beat, add the sugar a little at a time. When the mixture is pale, add the coffee, cognac, and nutmeg; stir well. Chill thoroughly and serve garnished with whole orange slices. Serve in punch cups or old-fashioned glasses.

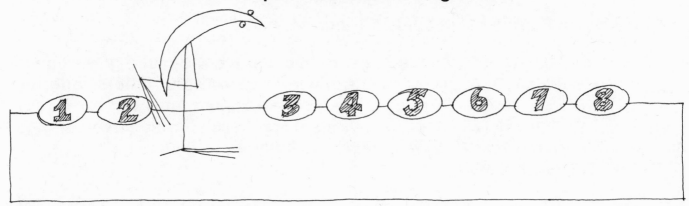

CHRISTMAS GLOGG   about 16 ½-cup servings

6 CARDOMOM SEEDS
10 CLOVES
2 STICKS CINNAMON
GRATED PEEL OF ½ ORANGE
3 CUPS CLARET
3 CUPS PORT
¼ CUP BLANCHED ALMONDS
½ CUP RAISINS
½ CUP PITTED PRUNES
1½ CUPS BRANDY
SUGAR CUBES

Tie the spices and orange peel in a piece of cheesecloth; pour claret and port into a kettle and immerse spice bag in it. Simmer mixture for 15 minutes; add almonds, raisins, and prunes, and simmer 15 minutes more. Remove spice bag and strain out the raisins, almonds, and prunes; discard. Pour the liquid into a heatproof punch bowl. In another utensil, pour the brandy over the sugar cubes and flame; pour immediately into the wine mixture. Serve in heated mugs or old-fashioned glasses into which spoons have been placed.

CLARET COOLER

about 12 ½-cup servings

2 TABLESPOONS SUGAR
2 TEASPOONS ANGOSTURA
BITTERS
GRATED PEEL OF 1 LEMON
1 TABLESPOON BRANDY
1 TABLESPOON WHITE
CURACAO
1 TABLESPOON MARASCHINO
LIQUEUR
1 STRIP CUCUMBER PEEL
1 FIFTH CHILLED RED WINE
2 CUPS CHILLED CLUB SODA
LEMON SLICES
PINEAPPLE SLICES
MINT SPRIGS

Combine all ingredients except the wine, soda, and garnishes and allow them to stand for 2 hours. Strain the mixture into a punch bowl over a block or ring of ice, add the wine and soda, and garnish with the fruit slices and mint sprigs. Serve in punch cups.

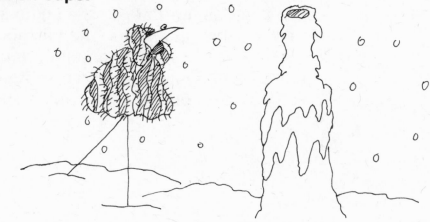

DESERT TONIC

about 12 ½-cup servings

1½ CUPS FRESH
ORANGE JUICE
1½ CUPS FRESH
GRAPEFRUIT JUICE
1 CUP FRESH TANGELO JUICE
¼ CUP TRIPLE SEC
2 CUPS TEQUILA
MINT SPRIGS

Combine all ingredients in a punch bowl over a block or ring of ice and garnish with mint sprigs. Serve in punch cups.

DUBONNET TINGLER   about 6-8 servings

2 CUPS CHILLED RED
DUBONNET
1 CUP CHILLED VODKA
JUICE AND CUT-UP PEEL
OF 3 LIMES
2 CUPS CHILLED CLUB SODA
MINT SPRIGS

Place all ingredients in a large glass pitcher filled with ice cubes and stir gently to mix. Serve in tall glasses filled with shaved ice and garnish with mint sprigs.
• Substitute gin for the vodka, if desired.

EGGNOG

12 EGGS, SEPARATED
¾ CUP SUGAR
1 QUART HALF AND HALF
1 CUP BLENDED WHISKEY *OR* BOURBON
1 CUP JAMAICA RUM *OR* BRANDY
3 CUPS HEAVY CREAM, WHIPPED
FRESHLY GRATED NUTMEG (OPTIONAL)
VANILLA OR HONEY ICE CREAM (OPTIONAL)

Beat egg yolks until thick. Add the sugar, a little at a time, continuing to beat until the mixture is pale in color. Continuing to beat constantly, add the half and half, whiskey, and rum in very small amounts at a time. Beat the egg whites until stiff and fold in gently. Then fold in the whipped cream very gently. Garnish with freshly grated nutmeg or a scoop of vanilla or honey ice cream, if desired. Serve in punch cups.

141

FISH HOUSE PUNCH

about 30 ½-cup servings

4 CUPS CONFECTIONERS
SUGAR
1 QUART LEMON JUICE
1 QUART JAMAICA RUM
1 FIFTH COGNAC
1 FIFTH WHITE WINE
½ CUP PEACH BRANDY

Dissolve sugar in a small amount of cold water and stir in the lemon juice. Pour over a block or ring of ice in a punch bowl and add remaining ingredients, stirring to mix well. Allow to stand undisturbed for several hours to mellow, stirring occasionally. Serve in punch cups.

GOLD DUST

about 6-8 servings

1½ CUPS TEQUILA
1½ CUPS TOMATO JUICE
1½ CUPS ORANGE JUICE
¼ CUP LEMON JUICE
2 TEASPOONS
WORCESTERSHIRE SAUCE
¼ CUP GRENADINE
DASH TABASCO SAUCE
SALT AND FRESHLY
GROUND PEPPER
LIME SLICES

Combine ingredients except lime slices and pour into a large, glass pitcher filled with ice cubes. Garnish with lime slices and serve in glasses with ice.

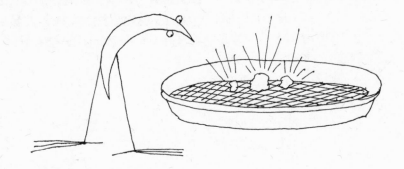

HOT BUTTERED CIDER

about 40 ½-cup servings

4 QUARTS SLIGHTLY TURNED
APPLE CIDER
¾ CUP FIRMLY PACKED
BROWN SUGAR
1 CUP BUTTER
2 CINNAMON STICKS,
EACH 2 INCHES LONG
10 CLOVES
1 QUART LIGHT RUM
ORANGE SLICES
WHOLE CLOVES

Heat the first five ingredients in a pan, stirring until the sugar is dissolved and the butter melted. Add rum; heat but do not boil. Pour into a heatproof punch bowl and garnish with thin orange slices studded with cloves. Serve in punch cups or mugs.
● Omit the rum for the children.

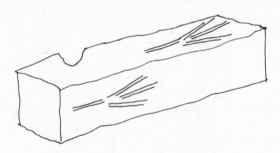

HOT TODDY BOWL   about 12 ½-cup servings

2 CUPS RUM
1 CINNAMON STICK,
2 INCHES LONG
1 LEMON, THINLY SLICED
8 CLOVES
2 TABLESPOONS SUGAR
4 CUPS BOILING WATER
CINNAMON STICKS
(OPTIONAL)
LEMON SLICES (OPTIONAL)

Combine all ingredients except the boiling water in a heatproof punch bowl, stirring to dissolve sugar. Add the boiling water, stir, and garnish with cinnamon sticks and lemon slices if desired. Serve in punch cups or mugs.

MAY WINE

4 BUNCHES SWEET
WOODRUFF
¾ CUP SUGAR
4 FIFTHS CHILLED WHITE WINE
1½ CUPS UNHULLED
STRAWBERRIES
2 FIFTHS CHILLED
CHAMPAGNE (OPTIONAL)

Place the woodruff in the bottom of a glass jar with a tight-fitting lid, add the sugar, cover the jar, and allow it to sit for several hours. Then fill the jar with wine, recover it tightly, and let the mixture stand overnight. Place a block or ring of ice in a punch bowl and pour the mixture in the jar over it; stir in the remainder of the wine and as many small, unhulled strawberries as desired. Finally, add the champagne if desired and serve in punch cups or champagne glasses.

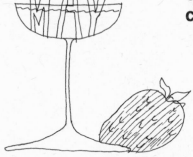

MIDSUMMER'S EVE BOWLE about 64 ½-cup servings

3 LEMONS
3 LIMES
1 RIPE PINEAPPLE, PEELED
2 CUPS SUGAR
1 QUART COGNAC
1 QUART CHILLED TEA
1 FIFTH CHILLED
JAMAICA RUM
1 FIFTH CHILLED
PEACH BRANDY
2 QUARTS CHILLED
CHAMPAGNE
2 QUARTS CHILLED
CLUB SODA

Thinly slice the lemons, limes, and pineapple. Sprinkle with sugar and marinate in cognac; refrigerate overnight. When ready to serve, place mixture in a punch bowl over a block or ring of ice and add the tea, rum, and peach brandy. Stir well and pour in the champagne and club soda. Serve in punch cups.

PARLOR CAR PUNCH   about 24 ½-cup servings

1½ CUPS SUGAR
8 EGGS
½ CUP MARASCHINO LIQUEUR
1 CUP CREME DE CACAO
1 TABLESPOON COINTREAU
1 QUART MILK
1 QUART CREAM
GRATED CHOCOLATE
ORANGE SLICES

Beat the sugar into the eggs until the mixture is thick and lemon-colored. Add the liqueurs, milk, and cream and pour over a block or ring of ice in a punch bowl. Garnish with grated chocolate and orange slices. Serve in punch cups.

PEACHES AND WINE PUNCH   about 10 servings

4 CUPS RED WINE
1 CUP LEMON JUICE
3 CUPS SLICED,
RIPE PEACHES
1½ CUPS SUGAR
½ TEASPOON GROUND
CINNAMON
8 CLOVES
8 WHOLE ALLSPICE
½ TEASPOON GINGER
SALT TO TASTE

Place all ingredients in a large glass pitcher filled with ice cubes and stir gently to mix. Chill thoroughly and then serve in glasses to which some of the peach slices have been added.

PINEAPPLE-LEMON FROST about 12–16 servings

2 CUPS WATER
1 TABLESPOON DRIED
ROSEMARY LEAVES
2 CUPS SUGAR
2 CUPS CHILLED LEMON JUICE
3 CUPS CHILLED
PINEAPPLE JUICE
SALT TO TASTE
3 CUPS CHILLED GIN
THIN LEMON SLICES

Place 2 cups water, the rosemary, and the sugar in a pan and bring to a boil; reduce heat and simmer 5 minutes, stirring constantly to dissolve the sugar. Remove the rosemary and discard. Allow the mixture to cool and then add the remaining ingredients except the lemon slices; chill. When ready to serve, pour over a block or ring of ice in a punch bowl and garnish with the lemon slices. Serve in tall glasses with ice.

ROMAN HOLIDAY PUNCH about 20 ½-cup servings

½ CUP LEMON JUICE
1 FIFTH CHILLED MARSALA
1 FIFTH CHILLED ROSE
1 FIFTH CHILLED BRANDY
RASPBERRY SHERBET
(OPTIONAL)

Mix all ingredients except the sherbet in a punch-bowl containing a block or ring of ice. Add scoops of sherbet, if desired. Serve in punch cups.

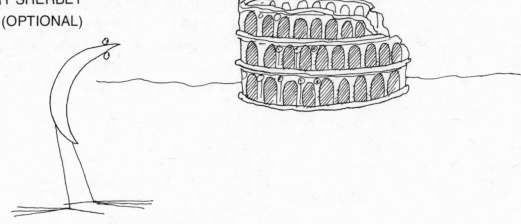

RUM CREAMS

about 40 ½-cup servings

1½ CUPS FIRMLY PACKED
BROWN SUGAR
½ CUP WATER
¼ CUP BUTTER
2 QUARTS MILK
1 QUART CREAM
¼ TEASPOON SALT
1 TABLESPOON VANILLA
EXTRACT
2 FIFTHS RUM
SWEETENED WHIPPED CREAM
GRATED ORANGE PEEL
FRESHLY GRATED NUTMEG

Add the brown sugar to ½ cup water in a large pan and bring it to a boil. Cook 5 minutes over low heat, stirring to dissolve the sugar. Add the butter, stirring occasionally until it has melted. Add the milk, cream, salt, and vanilla and heat; do not boil. Stir in the rum and heat very gently. Pour mixture into a heatproof punch bowl and garnish with dollops of whipped cream topped with grated orange peel and nutmeg. Serve in punch cups.

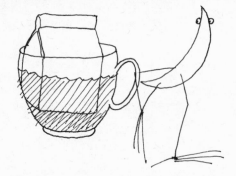

SANGRIA

about 16 servings

¼ CUP SUGAR
¼ CUP WATER
½ CUP LEMON JUICE
½ CUP ORANGE JUICE
2 TABLESPOONS COINTREAU
2 TABLESPOONS BRANDY
2 FIFTHS CHILLED RED WINE
1½ QUARTS CHILLED
CLUB SODA
LIME SLICES
THIN PEACH WEDGES

Place the sugar in a pan with the water and bring to a boil. Cook over low heat, stirring to dissolve the sugar, for 5 minutes; cool. Place the fruit juices, Cointreau, brandy, and red wine in a punch bowl filled with a block or ring of ice and stir in the sugar syrup. Pour in the club soda and garnish with fresh lime slices and peach wedges. Serve in tall glasses with ice.

WHITE SANGRIA: Substitute white wine for the red and fresh strawberries for the peach wedges.

SAUSALITO COCKTAIL   about 10-12 servings

1 QUART CHILLED TOMATO
JUICE, PREFERABLY FRESH
2 TABLESPOONS CHOPPED
GREEN PEPPER
1 CUP COARSELY CHOPPED
CELERY
2 TEASPOONS COARSELY
CHOPPED ONION
¼ CUP CUT-UP CUCUMBER
2 TABLESPOONS CHOPPED
PARSLEY
1 TABLESPOON CHOPPED
WATERCRESS
½ TEASPOON
WORCESTERSHIRE SAUCE
1 TABLESPOON LEMON JUICE

PINCH RED PEPPER
PINCH GARLIC POWDER
1 TEASPOON SALT
2 CUPS CHILLED VODKA
THIN LEMON SLICES

Place 1 cup of the tomato juice in the container of a blender with the remaining ingredients except the vodka and lemon slices. Blend until smooth and then add the remaining tomato juice. Pour into a punch bowl over a block or ring of ice, stir in the vodka, and garnish with the lemon slices. Serve in glasses with ice if desired.

154

SCOTCH N' LEMON   about 10 ½-cup servings

JUICE AND PEEL OF 6 LEMONS
½ CUP SUGAR
2 CUPS WATER
2 CUPS SCOTCH
LEMON-PEEL CURLS

Mix the lemon juice with the remaining ingredients; grate the lemon peels and add. Allow to stand for 24 hours, stirring occasionally. Strain out the peel and discard, pour the mixture over a block or ring of ice in a punch bowl, and garnish it with lemon curls. Serve in punch cups or old-fashioned glasses.

SEVILLE SUNSHINE

about 32 ½-cup servings

½ CUP SUGAR
1 CUP LEMON JUICE
4 CUPS CHILLED
ORANGE JUICE
1 CUP CHILLED COINTREAU
2 FIFTHS CHILLED WHITE WINE
1 QUART CHILLED CLUB SODA
ORANGE SLICES

Place the sugar in a pan with the lemon juice and bring it to a boil. Reduce the heat and cook 5 minutes, stirring to dissolve the sugar; cool. Then combine the lemon juice with the orange juice and pour over a block or ring of ice in a punch bowl; add the remaining ingredients, garnishing with the orange slices. Serve in punch cups.

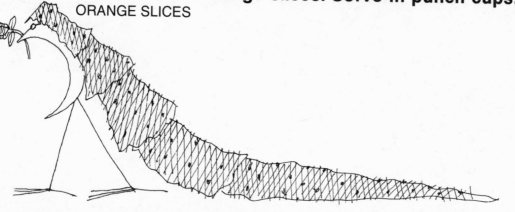

156

SOUTH SEAS SORCERER'S POTION about 20 servings

1 CUP SUGAR
½ CUP WATER
JUICE OF 1 LEMON
JUICE OF 2 ORANGES
1 CUP CRUSHED PINEAPPLE
½ TEASPOON ALMOND
EXTRACT
1 TEASPOON VANILLA
EXTRACT
8 RIPE BANANAS, MASHED
6 CUPS MILK
2 FIFTHS CHILLED RUM
PINEAPPLE SLICES
RED MARASCHINO CHERRIES
MINT LEAVES

Add the sugar to ½ cup water in a pan and bring to a boil. Cook over low heat 5 minutes, stirring to dissolve the sugar. Allow to cool and then mix with the fruit juices, pineapple, and extracts. Stir in the mashed bananas and then combine with the milk and rum. Pour over a block or ring of ice in a punch bowl and garnish with pineapple slices topped with cherries and mint sprigs. Serve in tall glasses.
● Serve in pineapple or coconut shells and garnish with fresh flowers and leaves, such as gardenias, to make this drink even more exotic.

SPARKLER

about 30 ½-cup servings

1 CUP COGNAC
½ CUP SUGAR
1 FIFTH CHILLED WHISKEY
1 FIFTH CHILLED WHITE WINE
2 QUARTS CHILLED CLUB
SODA
THIN LEMON, LIME,
AND ORANGE CURLS

Stir the sugar into the cognac to dissolve. Add the whiskey and wine and pour over a ring or block of ice in a punch bowl. Add the club soda and garnish with citrus curls. Serve in punch cups.

SUNDAY-BEST PUNCH   about 40 ½-cup servings

3 FIFTHS CHILLED RED WINE
2 CUPS DRY SHERRY
¼ CUP BRANDY
¼ CUP JAMAICA RUM
¼ CUP MARASCHINO LIQUEUR
¾ CUP LEMON JUICE
2 CUPS SUGAR
1 QUART CHILLED GINGER ALE
2 QUARTS CHILLED CLUB
SODA
LEMON SLICES
ORANGE SLICES

Eight hours or more before serving, combine the first 7 ingredients, stirring to dissolve the sugar, and refrigerate. When ready to serve, pour the mixture over a block or ring of ice in a punch bowl, add the ginger ale and club soda, and mix gently. Garnish with lemon and orange slices. Serve in punch cups.

159

SUNDOWN

about 60 ½-cup servings

1 FIFTH BRANDY
1 FIFTH SWEET VERMOUTH
⅓ CUP MARASCHINO LIQUEUR
½ CUP TRIPLE SEC
1½ QUARTS CHILLED
CLUB SODA
4 FIFTHS CHILLED
CHAMPAGNE
MANGO SLICES

Combine the brandy with the vermouth, Maraschino, and Triple Sec and pour over a ring or block of ice in a punch bowl. Add club soda and champagne and garnish with mango slices. Serve in punch cups.

SYLLABUB

about 8 ½-cup servings

1 CUP CHILLED WHITE WINE
JUICE AND GRATED PEEL
OF 1 LEMON
¾ CUP SUGAR
1½ CUPS MILK
1 CUP CREAM
2 EGG WHITES
FRESHLY GRATED NUTMEG

Combine the wine with the lemon juice and peel and ½ cup of the sugar; stir well to dissolve the sugar. Add the milk and cream, beating the mixture until frothy. Beat the egg whites until stiff, adding the remaining sugar a little at a time. Pour the wine mixture into a punch bowl and top with spoonfuls of the egg-white mixture. Sprinkle with nutmeg and serve in punch cups.

TOM AND JERRY

about 12–14 servings

12 EGGS
¾ CUP SUGAR
1 TEASPOON GROUND ALLSPICE
1 TEASPOON GROUND CINNAMON
SALT TO TASTE
1 CUP HOT JAMAICA RUM
2 CUPS HOT BOURBON
1 QUART HOT MILK
FRESHLY GRATED NUTMEG

Separate the eggs and beat the yolks until they begin to thicken. Then add the sugar gradually, continuing to beat until the mixture is thick and lemon-colored. Stir in the spices. Beat the egg whites with a dash of salt until stiff; gently fold into egg-yolk mixture. Add the rum and stir gently. To serve, place about 2 tablespoons of the mixture into each mug, add 2 tablespoons heated bourbon, and fill with hot milk. Top with freshly grated nutmeg.

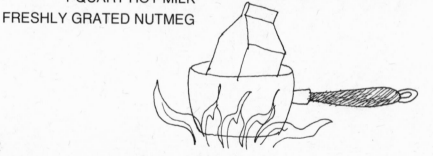

TROPICAL HAZE

about 20 ½-cup servings

½ CUP SUGAR
½ CUP WATER
2 CUPS CHILLED PINEAPPLE JUICE
1 CUP CHILLED CRANBERRY JUICE
1 CUP CHILLED ORANGE JUICE
2 CUPS CHILLED APPLE CIDER
2 TABLESPOONS LEMON JUICE
1 FIFTH CHILLED JAMAICA RUM
THIN PINEAPPLE SLICES
WHOLE CLOVES

Place the sugar in a pan with ½ cup water and bring it to a boil. Cook over low heat, stirring to dissolve the sugar, for 5 minutes. Allow to cool. Then combine the syrup with the remaining ingredients except the pineapple slices and cloves and pour over a block or ring of ice in a punch bowl. Stud the pineapple with the cloves and use to garnish the bowl. Serve in punch cups.

VINEYARD PUNCH

about 12–14 ½-cup servings

2 TABLESPOONS SUGAR
½ CUP WATER
2 CUPS CRANBERRY JUICE
2 CUPS APPLE JUICE
2 TABLESPOONS LEMON
JUICE
2 CUPS VODKA
THIN ORANGE SLICES
MINT SPRIGS

Place the sugar in a pan with the water and bring it to a boil. Cook 5 minutes over low heat, stirring to dissolve the sugar. Allow the mixture to cool. Add to the remaining ingredients except orange slices and mint sprigs and pour over a ring or block of ice in a punch bowl. Garnish with thin orange slices and mint sprigs. Serve in punch cups.

WASSAIL BOWL

about 24 ½-cup servings

2 QUARTS APPLE CIDER
1 CUP FIRMLY PACKED
BROWN SUGAR
½ CUP ORANGE JUICE
½ CUP LEMON JUICE
1 TEASPOON WHOLE
ALLSPICE
2 TEASPOONS WHOLE
CLOVES
2 STICKS CINNAMON,
EACH 2 INCHES LONG
1 TEASPOON GROUND
NUTMEG
1 TABLESPOON GROUND
GINGER
SALT TO TASTE

2 CUPS JAMAICA RUM *OR*
APPLE BRANDY
WHOLE SPICED CRAB APPLES

Combine all ingredients except the rum and crab apples in a kettle, bring the mixture to a boil, and simmer about 10 minutes. Pour mixture through a sieve into another pan, add rum, and heat; do not boil. Pour into a heatproof punch bowl and garnish with whole spiced crab apples. Serve in punch cups.

Nonalcoholic Punches

CAFE OLE!

about 10 servings

2 OUNCES UNSWEETENED
CHOCOLATE
¼ CUP SUGAR
PINCH SALT
2 CUPS MILK
2 CUPS CREAM
1 TEASPOON VANILLA
EXTRACT
4 CUPS HOT ESPRESSO
SWEETENED WHIPPED CREAM
GRATED ORANGE PEEL
CINNAMON STICKS,
EACH 3 INCHES LONG

Stirring constantly, heat the first 5 ingredients in a pan until milk is hot (not boiling) and chocolate is melted. Stir in vanilla and espresso and pour into large mugs. Top with whipped cream sprinkled with grated orange peel and add cinnamon-stick stirrers.

CANDY CANE NOG

about 24 ½-cup servings

6 EGGS, SEPARATED
1 QUART CHILLED CREAM
¾ CUP CRUSHED PEPPERMINT
CANDY CANES
1 QUART VANILLA ICE CREAM,
SOFTENED
1 QUART GINGER ALE
SWEETENED WHIPPED CREAM
SMALL CANDY CANES

Beat the egg yolks until thick and lemon-colored. Stir in the cream and ½ cup of the candy. Beat egg whites until stiff and fold in gently. Place scoops of vanilla ice cream in a punch bowl and pour in the punch mixture; add ginger ale. Top with dollops of whipped cream sprinkled with the remaining crushed candy. Serve in punch cups with candy-cane stirrers.

CITRUS JULEPS   about 30 servings

1 CUP MINT LEAVES
1 CUP WATER
1 CUP SUGAR
1½ QUARTS GRAPEFRUIT JUICE
2 CUPS CHILLED ORANGE JUICE
2 CUPS CHILLED TANGERINE JUICE
1 CUP CHILLED PINEAPPLE JUICE
½ CUP CHILLED LEMON JUICE
1 QUART CHILLED CLUB SODA
1 QUART CHILLED GINGER ALE
MINT SPRIGS
LIME SLICES

Bruise the mint leaves gently with the back of a spoon and place in a pan along with the water and sugar. Bring to a boil; reduce heat and cook gently for 5 minutes, stirring to dissolve the sugar. Strain out the mint leaves and discard; allow mixture to cool. Combine mixture with the fruit juices in a punch bowl over a block or ring of ice; fill with club soda and ginger ale. Garnish with mint sprigs and lime slices. Serve in tall glasses with crushed ice.

169

CLASSIC CAPPUCCINO   about 6–8 servings

3 CUPS HOT MILK
3 CUPS HOT ESPRESSO
NUTMEG
CINNAMON STICKS
SUGAR

Fill each of 6 cups with half milk and half espresso. Sprinkle with nutmeg, freshly grated if possible. Add cinnamon-stick stirrers and sweeten to taste.
● **Top with dollops of sweetened whipped cream garnished with grated chocolate, if desired.**

COFFEE FRAPPE   about 6 servings

4 CUPS STRONG COFFEE
1 CINNAMON STICK,
2 INCHES LONG, BROKEN UP
NUTMEG
2 TEASPOONS ANGOSTURA
BITTERS
1 TABLESPOON SUGAR
1 PINT COFFEE ICE CREAM,
SOFTENED

Place coffee with broken-up cinnamon stick, nutmeg (preferably freshly ground), bitters, and sugar in a pan and heat gently for a few minutes, stirring to dissolve sugar. Remove and discard the cinnamon; chill the mixture. Then place the mixture in a bowl with the ice cream and beat until smooth. Pour into tall glasses to serve.

FRUIT FIZZ

about 20 ½-cup servings

1 PINT (1½ CUPS)
RASPBERRIES
1 CUP SUGAR
4 CUPS CHILLED
PINEAPPLE JUICE
½ CUP LEMON JUICE
1 QUART CHILLED GINGER ALE
MINT SPRIGS

Wash raspberries and press them through a sieve to purée; discard seeds. Place sugar in a pan with the fruit juices and bring to a boil. Cook gently over low heat, stirring to dissolve sugar, for 5 minutes; cool mixture. Stir in raspberry purée and pour over a block or ring of ice in a punch bowl. Fill with ginger ale and garnish with mint sprigs. Serve in punch cups.

FRUIT SHRUB   about 8 servings

½ CUP SUGAR
½ CUP WATER
8 CLOVES
1 STICK CINNAMON,
2 INCHES LONG
1 CUP CHILLED GRAPEFRUIT
JUICE
1 CUP CHILLED PINEAPPLE
JUICE
1 CUP CHILLED APRICOT
NECTAR
1 CUP CHILLED ORANGE JUICE
ORANGE SHERBET

Place sugar, water, cloves, and cinnamon in a saucepan and bring to a boil. Reduce heat and simmer 5 minutes, stirring to dissolve sugar. Remove cloves and cinnamon and discard. Combine with the remaining ingredients, except sherbet. To serve, place a scoop of sherbet in each glass and fill with the fruit mixture.

HANSEL AND GRETEL PUNCH   about 20 ½-cup servings

1 QUART CHILLED EGGNOG
1 PINT CHERRY-VANILLA
ICE CREAM
1 QUART CHILLED
CHERRY SODA
SWEETENED WHIPPED CREAM
SHAVED CHOCOLATE
RED MARASCHINO CHERRIES,
CUT UP

Pour eggnog into a punch bowl and add scoops of cherry-vanilla ice cream. Pour in the cherry soda and add puffs of whipped cream. Garnish the whipped cream with shaved chocolate and bits of cherries.

HOT CHOCOLATE MEXICANO   about 10 servings

3 EGG WHITES
½ CUP COCOA POWDER
1 CUP SUGAR
4 CINNAMON STICKS, EACH
1 INCH LONG
¼ TEASPOON SALT
2 QUARTS MILK
10 CINNAMON STICKS, EACH
3 INCHES LONG (OPTIONAL)

Beat the egg whites until stiff. Place the cocoa powder in a pan with the sugar, cinnamon, salt, and 1 cup of the milk. Cook over low heat, stirring constantly, until the cocoa powder and sugar are dissolved. Add the rest of the milk and bring just to boiling point. Remove from heat, remove cinnamon sticks, and beat the mixture until frothy. Gradually add the beaten egg whites while continuing to beat the chocolate mixture. When mixture is very frothy, serve in cups with cinnamon-stick stirrers, if desired.

174

MEDITERRANEAN ADE   about 8 ½-cup servings

¼ CUP SUGAR
1¼ CUPS LEMON JUICE
2 CUPS ORANGE JUICE
½ CUP WHITE GRAPE JUICE
1 TABLESPOON CREAM
RED RASPBERRIES
(OPTIONAL)

Place the sugar with ¼ cup of the lemon juice in a pan and bring to a boil. Cook over low heat, stirring to dissolve the sugar, for 5 minutes; cool the mixture. Add the remaining ingredients except the raspberries and pour over a block or ring of ice in a punch bowl. Garnish with red raspberries, if desired. Serve in punch cups or glasses with crushed ice.

MINT TEA JULEPS   about 6 ½-cup servings

1 CUP MINT LEAVES
1 CUP HOT, STRONG TEA
1 CUP SUGAR
1 CUP WATER
2 TABLESPOONS LEMON
JUICE
MINT SPRIGS
LEMON SLICES

Bruise the mint leaves gently with the back of a spoon and steep them in the hot tea. In the meantime, place the sugar and water in a large pan and bring to a boil. Reduce heat and cook gently, stirring to dissolve sugar, for 5 minutes; cool mixture. Stir in the lemon juice. When the tea has cooled, strain out the mint leaves and discard. Combine the mixture with the sugar syrup and pour it over a block or ring of ice in a punch bowl. Garnish with mint sprigs and lemon slices. Serve in glasses with crushed ice.

OLD-FASHIONED LEMONADE about 12–14 servings

5 LEMONS
1 ORANGE
2 CUPS SUGAR
6 CUPS COLD WATER
1 TABLESPOON FRESH
ROSEMARY LEAVES
(½ TEASPOON DRIED)
ROSEMARY SPRIGS
(OPTIONAL)

Squeeze the lemons and orange and set juice aside. Grate one of the lemon peels and combine it with the sugar, 2 cups of the water, and the rosemary in a pan. Bring the mixture to a boil and cook over low heat 5 minutes, stirring to dissolve the sugar. Strain out the rosemary leaves and allow the mixture to cool. Add the remaining 4 cups cold water and serve in tall glasses filled with cracked ice; garnish with fresh rosemary sprigs.

PINK BUBBLY STUFF (MOCK PINK CHAMPAGNE)   about 30 ½-cup servings

1 CUP SUGAR
2 CUPS WATER
3 CUPS CHILLED ORANGE JUICE
1½ CUPS CHILLED PINEAPPLE JUICE
1½ CUPS CHILLED GRAPEFRUIT JUICE
1 CUP CHILLED LIME JUICE
½ CUP GRENADINE, OR TO TASTE
DASH NUTMEG
1 QUART GINGER ALE
STRAWBERRIES

Place sugar in a pan with the water and bring to a boil. Lower heat and cook 5 minutes, stirring to dissolve sugar. Remove from heat and allow to cool. Combine with the fruit juices, grenadine, and nutmeg and pour over a block or ring of ice in a punch bowl. Fill with ginger ale and garnish with strawberries. Serve in champagne glasses.

ST. PATRICK'S DAY PUNCH   about 30 ½-cup servings

2 CANS (6 OUNCES EACH)
LIMEADE CONCENTRATE
8 MINT SPRIGS
2 QUARTS CHILLED LIME SODA
1 QUART LIME SHERBET
GREEN MARASCHINO
CHERRIES

Prepare the limeade according to the directions on the can. Remove the leaves from the mint sprigs and bruise them gently with the back of a spoon; mix them with the limeade and allow to stand for several hours. Remove the leaves and pour into a punch bowl over a block or ring of ice. Add lime soda and garnish with scoops of lime sherbet. Cut the cherries in halves to make a four-leaved shamrock on top of each scoop of sherbet; cut several halves in strips to make stems. Serve in punch cups.

SPICED TOMATO BOWL   about 16–18 ½-cup servings

2 QUARTS TOMATO JUICE,
PREFERABLY FRESH
SALT AND FRESHLY GROUND
PEPPER TO TASTE
½ CUP SUGAR
¼ CUP LEMON JUICE
⅛ TEASPOON GROUND
NUTMEG
⅛ TEASPOON GROUND
CINNAMON
⅛ TEASPOON GROUND
CLOVES
THIN LEMON SLICES

Combine all ingredients except lemon slices in a pan and bring to a boil. Cook 5 minutes over low heat, stirring to dissolve sugar. Chill and pour into punch bowl over block or ring of ice. Garnish with lemon slices and serve in punch cups.

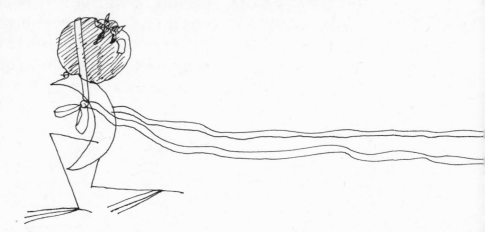

SYLLABUB (NONALCOHOLIC)   about 16 ½-cup servings

JUICE AND GRATED PEEL
OF 1 LEMON
2 CUPS CHILLED APPLE JUICE
1 CUP SUGAR
3 CUPS MILK
2 CUPS CREAM
4 EGG WHITES
NUTMEG

Mix the lemon juice and peel with the apple juice and half the sugar, stirring well to dissolve the sugar. Add the milk and cream, beating until frothy. Beat the egg whites until stiff, adding the remaining sugar a little at a time, and fold into the milk mixture. Pour into a punch bowl over a block or ring of ice and sprinkle with nutmeg, preferably freshly grated. Serve in punch cups.

VIENNESE COFFEE

about 6–8 servings

6 CUPS STRONG COFFEE
2 TEASPOONS GRATED
ORANGE PEEL
SWEETENED WHIPPED CREAM
NUTMEG

Place coffee in a pan; tie grated orange peel in a place of cheesecloth and submerge in the coffee. Heat pan over a low flame until coffee is very hot but not boiling. Remove orange peel and pour coffee into mugs. Top with whipped cream sprinkled with nutmeg, preferably freshly ground.

Glossary

ABSINTHE: An anise-flavored liqueur made with wormwood; illegal in most countries, including the United States. Absinthe substitutes include Abisante, anisette, Herbsaint, Pernod.

AMARETTO: A liqueur made from apricot pits; it has a sweet, nutty flavor.

AMER PICON: A bitter French aperitif liqueur, flavored with oranges, quinine, and spices.

ANISETTE: An anise-flavored liqueur.

APPLEJACK: Apple brandy with a pronounced apple flavor.

ARMAGNAC: A brandy similar to cognac, though somewhat drier, produced only in France's Armagnac region.

BEER: The general term for five types of malt beverage; the lightest, lager, is also the most popular. Ale is somewhat darker and has a bit more "bite." Bock, porter, and stout are progressively darker, sweeter, and richer.

BENEDICTINE: An herb- and spice-flavored brandy made from a secret recipe created by Benedictine monks.

BITTERS: Aromatic, bitter blends of roots, herbs, berries, barks, and spices. The three most common kinds are Angostura, orange, and Peychaud's.

BOURBON: A whiskey distilled from mash that was at least 51 percent corn grain.

BRANDY: A liquor made by distilling a mash of fermented grapes or other fruits. Used alone, the term refers to brandy made from grapes.

BYRRH: An aromatic French aperitif wine.

CALVADOS: French apple brandy.

CAMPARI: A slightly bitter Italian apertif liqueur, often served with club soda and a twist of lemon.

CHARTREUSE: A liqueur originated by the Carthusian monks of France. Green Chartreuse is 110 proof; yellow, 86 proof.

CHERRY LIQUEUR: Cherry-flavored cordials are sold as cherry-flavored brandy, Cherry Heering, Cherry Karise, and crème de cerise.

CLARISTINE: An herb-flavored liqueur originated by the Clarist nuns of Belgium.

COBBLER: A drink mixed in a tall glass or large goblet that has been packed with crushed or finely cracked ice. The drink is not diluted with anything other than small amounts of fruit juice.

COFFEE LIQUEUR: Coffee-flavored cordials are sold as Brazilia, crème de café, Espresso, Kahlúa, Pasha, and Tia Maria.

COGNAC: A kind of brandy made in the region around the city of Cognac, France.

COINTREAU: An orange-flavored liqueur.

COLLINS: A type of fizz, made with lemon juice, sugar, liquor, and club soda. The two most common are the tom collins, made with gin, and the john collins, made with geneva (Dutch gin).

COOLER: A tall, warm-weather drink, similar to a cobbler except that sparkling beverages are added.

CORDIAL: A term synonymous with *liqueur;* these are liquors made by adding infusions of fruits, barks, berries, herbs, spices, flowers, roots, and sweetening to bases of grain alcohol, brandy, or whiskey. Usually served as after-dinner drinks.

CREME DE CACAO: A brandy-based liqueur, flavored with cocoa beans, vanilla beans, and spices. Available in both white and brown types.

CREME DE CASSIS: A liqueur made from black currants, it's very popular in the vermouth cassis, the white-wine (*vin-blanc*) cassis, and the kir.

CREME DE MENTHE: A peppermint-flavored liqueur available in white, green, or red versions.

CREME DE NOYAUX: An almond-flavored liqueur.

CREME DE ROSE: A rose-flavored liqueur.

CREME DE VANILLE: A vanilla-flavored liqueur.

CREME DE VIOLETTE: A liqueur flavored with vanilla and violet petals.

CREME D'YVETTE: A proprietary liqueur similar to crème de violette, but with a stronger violet bouquet.

CURACAO: A liqueur made from the peel of oranges grown on the island of Curaçao in the Dutch West Indies. Usually orange in color, it is also available in white and blue versions.

DAISY: A kind of large cocktail, daisies are almost always sweetened with raspberry syrup or grenadine and are served in a stein or metal cup.

DRAMBUIE: A liqueur made from Scotch whisky, herbs, and honey.

DUBONNET: An aromatic French aperitif wine with a slight quinine taste. Available in both red and white.

FALERNUM: A syrup from the West Indies, flavored with almonds and spices.

FERNET BRANCA: An aromatic used for flavoring in cocktails and as an aperitif.

FIX: A smaller version of the cobbler.

FIZZ: A tall drink suitable for warm weather or brunches. Fizzes are usually made of lemon or lime juice and club soda; some fizz recipes call for an egg white.

FLIP: A drink especially well-suited for beginning or ending the day. Flips are similar to eggnogs and are usually served with grated nutmeg on top.

FRAISE: Strawberry brandy.

FRAISETTE: A strawberry-flavored liqueur.

FRAMBOISE: A clear raspberry brandy.

FRAPPE: A drink made by pouring a liqueur over crushed ice, usually in a tall glass.

GALLIANO LIQUORE: An Italian liqueur, golden in color, flavored with vanilla, anise, and herbs.

GIN: A liquor distilled from grain and flavored with juniper berries and various other botanicals. Dry gin or London dry gin is the most popular in this country. Vacuum-distilled gins tend to be gentler and subtler than other gins. Old Tom Gin is an English gin that has been sweetened. Hollands, geneva, and Schiedam, from Holland, and Steinhäger, from Germany, are highly flavored and usually taken straight; they do not mix well with other ingredients.

GRAND MARNIER: A French liqueur with a cognac base and an orange flavor.

GRENADINE: A sweet, nonalcoholic syrup made from pomegranates and used in a great many cocktails and punches.

IRISH MIST: A liqueur made from Irish whiskey and honey.

IRISH WHISKEY: A full-bodied whiskey, usually 86 proof, distilled in Ireland and made up of a blend of grain whiskies and barley malt whiskies.

187

KIRSCH: A colorless cherry brandy.

KUMMEL: A caraway-flavored liqueur.

LILLET: A somewhat bitter, orange-flavored French apéritif wine; available in both white and red.

MARASCHINO: A colorless, bittersweet, cherry liqueur.

MIST: A drink made by pouring straight liquor, such as Scotch, over crushed ice, usually in an old-fashioned glass. Often served with a twist of fruit peel.

ORGEAT; ORZATA: Nonalcoholic, almond-flavored syrups, from France and Italy, respectively.

OUZO: An anise-flavored liqueur from Greece, it can be served in a cordial glass, on the rocks straight, or on the rocks mixed with a little water. Ouzo turns milky when mixed with water.

PASTIS: An anise-flavored liqueur from France.

PEPPERMINT SCHNAPPS: A mint-flavored brandy; similar to crème de menthe, but more potent and less sweet.

PERNOD: A French, anise-flavored liqueur; the most common absinthe substitute.

PRUNELLE: A plum-flavored liqueur.

PUNT E MES: A somewhat bitter Italian apéritif wine with a dark color.

QUININE WATER: Also called tonic water, quinine water is the mixer used in gin and tonic, vodka and tonic, and other, usually warm-weather, drinks.

RAKI: A potent, anise-flavored brandy from the Middle East.

REISHU: A melon liqueur from the Orient.

RICKEYS: Highballs made with liquor, club soda, and fresh lime.

RUM: A liquor distilled from the fermented juice of sugar cane. There are three basic types of rum: light, golden, and dark. Light rum is the most versatile and can be substituted for almost any liquor in nearly any recipe. Golden rum is used in the classic Cuba libre (rum and coke), as well as a number of other drinks with a slightly more pronounced rum flavor. Dark rums, which are heavier and more molasses-like, are used almost exclusively in tropical fruit-juice drinks and punches.

SCOTCH WHISKY: A liquor distilled in Scotland, Scotch contains both barley malt whiskies and grain whiskies. The distinctive, smoky flavor of Scotch comes from peat fires used in its production. Although usually taken straight on the rocks or with water or club soda, Scotch also combines well with other ingredients to make a number of cock-tails.

SLOE GIN: A liqueur flavored with sloes, the fruit of the blackthorn bush.

SOUTHERN COMFORT: A bourbon-based, peach-flavored American liqueur.

STREGA: A yellowish liqueur from Italy; its flavor comes from a combination of roots, herbs, and berries.

SWEDISH PUNCH: Also known as arrack punsch and caloric punsch. A pale yellow liqueur from Sweden, it has a flavor reminiscent of rum and citrus.

TEQUILA: A clear liquor from Mexico made from the century plant.

TRIPLE SEC: A clear, orange-flavored liqueur, similar to Cointreau and Curaçao, though somewhat less sweet.

TUACA: A milky, orange-flavored brandy from Italy.

TWIST: Many drink recipes call for a twist of fruit peel: When the drink has been mixed, squeeze and twist the peel over the glass to release the aromatic oils and then drop the peel into the glass. For a stronger fruit flavor, rub the rim of the glass with the peel before dropping it into the drink.

VERMOUTH: A dark (sweet) or light (dry) aperitif wine containing a total of several dozen barks, berries, herbs, spices, and seeds. Although essential ingredients in a number of cocktails, both sweet and dry vermouth are often served on the rocks with a twist of fruit peel.

VODKA: Because it is very nearly odorless and tasteless, vodka is perhaps the most versatile of liquors. Originally made in Russia from potatoes, it is now usually distilled from fermented grains. In the United States, vodka must be at least 80 proof (40 percent alcohol).

WHISKEY: A general name for any liquor distilled from a fermented mash of grain, such as barley, corn, rye, or wheat.

Index